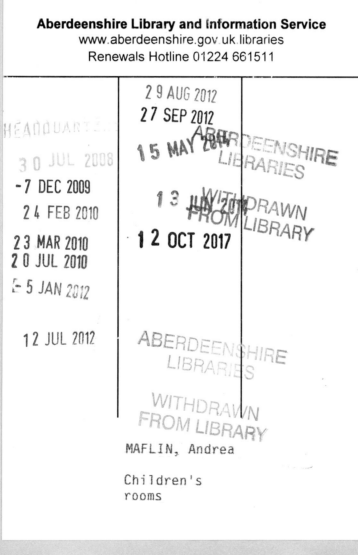

children's
rooms

children's
rooms

Great ideas to transform your child's space plus 25 step-by-step projects

Andrea Maflin

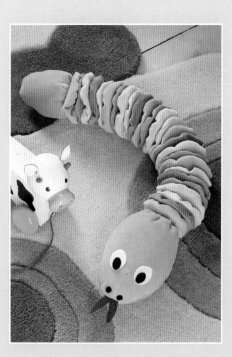

CICO BOOKS

London New York

To my friends Hilda and John Laity, whose warmth, kindness and generosity of spirit resonates, but most of all I applaud them for their mischievous, fun-loving natures

First published in 2008 by CICO Books
an imprint of Ryland Peters & Small
20–21 Jockey's Fields, London WC1R 4BW

www.cicobooks.co.uk

10 9 8 7 6 5 4 3 2 1

Text © Andrea Maflin 2008
Design and photography © CICO Books 2008

A CIP catalogue record for this book is available from the British Library.

ISBN-13: 978 1 906094 35 5
ISBN-10: 1 906094 35 7

Printed in China

Editor Kate Haxell
Designer Claire Legemah
Photographer Christopher Drake
Illustrator Stephen Dew

contents

introduction

Creating a room for a child is part of the fun of having a family. Every child is an individual, but some design ideas will entrance many little ones, and also captivate their parents.

I love spending time with children – their curiosity, humour and instinctive reactions never fail to delight – and I equally enjoy designing rooms for them, using my skills to translate their loves and ideas into design schemes that suit them, and also work for their parents. In this book I hope to show you how, with just a little know-how, some imagination and not too much money, you can create a special room for your child. If children see a room as their own space, they love to spend time in it. Whether your child is a one-month-old baby girl or an eight-year-old boy, and whatever decorative tastes you may share, I hope that there is something here to inspire you to start your own decorating adventure.

planning

You almost can't do too much of this. Start early and by the time the baby arrives you will have a room ready to welcome your newborn into the world. Firstly, measure the room you have chosen for your child and make a scale drawing of the space. This need not be a work of art, but it must be accurate. Then draw in, to scale, any pieces of furniture you already have for the room. Now you can go on to choose the rest.

vintage
Turn to page 28 for ideas on decorating a nursery in vintage style.

spotty
On page 96 you will find inspiration for a playroom for boys and girls alike.

design

Remember that just because this is a room for a child, it doesn't have to be traditionally childish. You don't have to sacrifice your own tastes and design ideas if you don't want to – there is no reason why this room shouldn't be decoratively as much a part of your home as any other room. Especially when designing a nursery for a baby, you can stamp your own ideas on it, confident that the room will evolve naturally as the child grows. If the room is for an older child, talk to him or her about it. Children often have surprisingly strong opinions and it's a good plan to take them into account.

Gather together cuttings from magazines, ideas from books and pictures of products you love and see where that collection leads you. An overriding theme or style may well come to the fore. Try to avoid this year's fad ideas because they will date quickly and you, and your child, will tire of them equally quickly.

details
There are projects and ideas for every part of a room, from framed keepsakes to lampshades.

budget

Few people have unlimited funds for decorating a child's room, so you'll find plenty of ideas in this book for recycling and making the most of existing and inexpensive pieces. Set your budget at the start of the project and keep to it. You've planned what you will need, so resist buying a gorgeous sleigh bed if the look you are going for is colourful and naive. However, remember to balance cost against longevity – an expensive buy might be worth it if the piece will last ten years.

Don't start out by buying everything you think you may ever need, even though this is tempting, particularly with a first child. As you will see in Nursery Colour (page 82), an uncluttered room with minimal furnishings can work very well. Start by buying only what you absolutely need now – you can always get more things later when and if you require them.

◀ colour

An important part of any design scheme, colour can be a starting point for your nursery ideas.

themes

It's better to choose a classic motif rather than a specific character – spacemen and spaceships are often popular with boys.

playroom
On page 56 you will find lovely ideas for a boy's den and on page 96, more design inspiration for a playroom.

fun
Creative play is important to a child, so a space where they can put together masterpieces without damaging your furnishings is ideal.

function

Your room scheme has to depend on what the room is to be used for. If it is just a nursery, it needs little more than a cot, storage space and a comfortable chair for you. If it is a bedroom that will also be the main play area, a few more practical requirements have to be taken into account. As well as accommodating the child and his or her clothes, storage for toys and hobby materials will have to be included. If you have enough space for a separate bedroom and playroom, apply separate principles to each one. Whatever the room is to be, I hope you will find a multitude of ideas for it in this book.

boho chic

Don't abandon your personal design style when planning a nursery. This boho-themed, yet calm room fits in with a glamorous interior scheme in the rest of the home.

A calm nursery doesn't have to be a dull one. Light colours and reflective surfaces, with accents of stronger pastel colours introduced through accessories, create a relaxing and practical room that can be easily adapted as your child grows. The large-scale print of the wallpaper makes a design statement, but the soft, muted silver and gold tones don't overpower the space. You are going to spend a good deal of time in this room, so it needs to be a space where you feel relaxed and comfortable.

sleep

A cot is a major purchase, so take the time over your choice. The baby will probably sleep in your room for the first six months, and a cot with an adjustable mattress position can make night feeds easier for mother and child. This type of cot will be suitable until the baby is about two years old. A cot bed that is suitable for a child from birth up to five years old is also a great investment. Position the bed where it's not in the path of direct sunlight, or next to a heater, and make sure that the windows can be blacked out for day-time naps – a blackout blind plus lined curtains are a practical and stylish solution.

flexible storage
Choose pieces that can be used for different items as your child grows. This shelving unit, for instance, holds toys and clothes for a young baby, but it will serve equally well for school bags and gym kit as the child grows up.

lighting

You need at least two sorts of light in the room: a bright light that lets you see clearly for nappy-changing and cleaning up, and a low-level light that you can turn on at night to see what you are doing, without waking the baby. Consider a table lamp fitted with a low-wattage bulb, or have a dimmer switch fitted to the overhead light. Alternatively, fairy lights fixed securely along the picture rail provide soft light and, as there are so many different styles available now, you are bound to be able to find something lovely to suit the room.

toys, toys, toys
These must be practical, but that doesn't mean they have to be boring or ugly. This crochet dog is baby-safe, washable, and very cute.

the room

Various practical considerations, as well as style and design, have to be taken into account in a nursery. One vital ingredient is good, flexible storage, and lots of it. Built-in wardrobes are a great idea and will remain useful for some years. A well-made chest of drawers is a good investment, especially if the top is the right height for a nappy-changing station, and lined baskets (see pages 22–3 for instructions) are useful for all sorts of baby bits and pieces.

A nursing mother needs a really comfortable chair that she can sit in for long sessions, without aches and pains. Scatter cushions that can be used to prop elbows and support backs are a good idea. Windows must be fully curtained so day-time naps are possible, and the cot must be away from direct sunlight or the baby will get too hot very quickly. You need heating for cold weather, but it must be baby-safe with guards on heaters and covers on radiators.

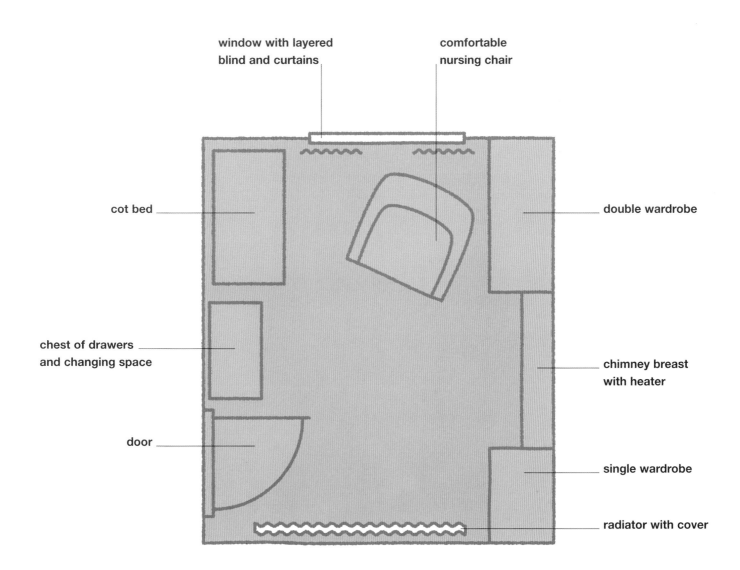

window with layered blind and curtains

comfortable nursing chair

cot bed

double wardrobe

chest of drawers and changing space

chimney breast with heater

door

single wardrobe

radiator with cover

pussycat soft toy

Raid your scrapbag for pieces of patterned fabric to make this cuddly little cat. I've left its little face plain to show off how charming it is, full of whiskers and eyelashes. The pattern pieces are all on pages 126–7. You can use them the size they are, or if you want to make a bigger toy, just use a photocopier to enlarge the pieces, all by the same amount, and cut out your paper patterns.

you will need
- Templates on pages 126–7
- Patterned and plain fabrics
- Pins
- Scissors
- Sewing machine
- Sewing thread
- Hand-sewing needle
- Washable toy stuffing
- Embroidery thread
- Embroidery needle

1 Cut out two bibs and two front bodies. Appliqué the bib pieces to the front of the body pieces with a zigzag stitch. Using straight stitch, machine the two pieces together. Cut two back bodies and join them in the same way.

2 Cut one tail piece. Fold in half lengthways, right side facing; stitch the long edge. Turn right side out. Lightly stuff. Run a gathering thread along the seam to the end and pull it up to curl the tail. Hand-sew to the back body seam.

3 Cut out four arms and four legs. Pin pairs of pieces together and, with right sides facing, stitch around the edges, leaving the tops open. Turn right side out and stuff them, leaving the top 2.5cm (1in.) empty.

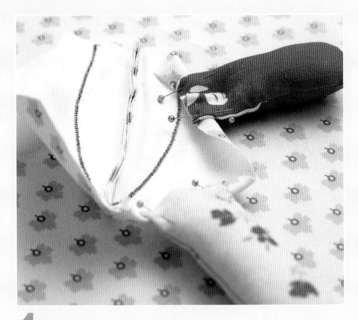

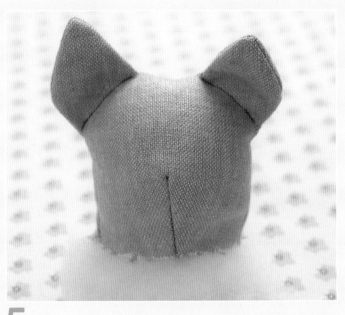

4 Pin the arms and legs in position on the right side of the front body. Right sides facing, pin the back body to the front and stitch all around, trapping the arms and legs into the seams and leaving the neck open. Stuff the body.

5 Stitch the dart in the front of the head, then, right sides facing, stitch the back of the head to the front; turn right side out. Stitch across the base of the ears so that when the head is stuffed, the ears remain flat. Then stuff the head firmly.

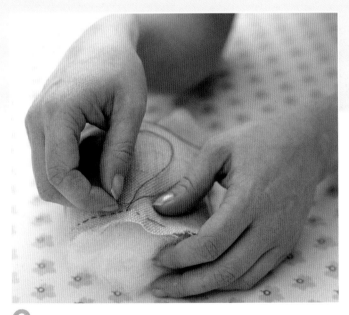

6 Run a gathering stitch around the neck edge of the head. Pull up the thread so that the neck fits to the top of the body. Making sure that the side seams line up, hand-sew the head to the body.

7 Embroider the face and paws, using three strands of embroidery thread.

toys

When babies are small they will play with almost anything, including things you would prefer them not to touch! So choose toys that are lovely and tactile, colourful and appealing and that you like the look of. Nursery toys can be great design statements and there are many gorgeous ones to choose from. Always check the labelling on a toy to make sure it is suitable for your baby's age and is easily cleaned, either by putting it through the washing machine or by wiping off. If you are making toys for your baby, buy proper, washable stuffing and sew everything securely.

colour and texture
Babies love bright colours and stripes and patterns that help them to focus their eyes. Plush fabrics and crinkly textures are popular with little fingers.

panelled wardrobe door

The fitted wardrobes in this nursery have completely flat doors that do not complement the style of

the Victorian house, which has panelled doors and many decorative details. However, it isn't difficult

to embellish the doors so that they fit in with the styling of the rest of the house. I've used soft

pearlescent wallpaper within the beading to add an extra accent to this baby girl's nursery.

you will need
- Door
- Tape measure
- Pencil
- Wooden beading
- Saw
- Mitre box
- Wood glue
- Panel pins
- Hammer
- Primer
- Paintbrush
- Varnish roller
- Roller tray
- Water-based eggshell paint
- Wallpaper and paste (optional)
- Water-based varnish (optional)

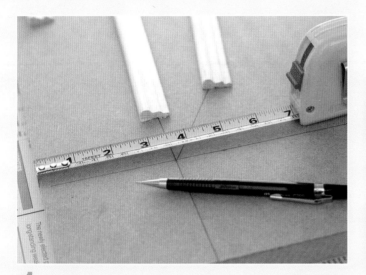

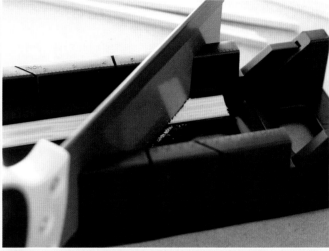

1 Take the door off the hinges and measure and mark out the panel on the front of it. Here I have elected to replace the entire door and so have had a piece of suitable MDF cut to size. Look at and measure other doors in the house to help you judge the width of the border around the beading.

2 Using the saw and mitre box, cut lengths of beading to fit the marked-up door. Each length must have 45° ends so that the corners join neatly.

3 Run a line of glue along the back of each piece of beading and position them on the drawn lines. Hammer in a panel pin at the end of each length, then leave the door flat to dry overnight.

TIP If you have a wall that is completely covered with fitted wardrobes, choose a wallpaper for the panels that has a large-scale pattern to add splashes of drama. Avoid mini patterns if the room is small, because they could make the room seem too busy.

4 Choose primer suitable for the surface: melamine requires a special primer to prevent the paint scratching off. Using the paintbrush and roller, prime the door and leave to dry. Finish with two coats of eggshell paint. If you want to wallpaper the central panel, paint the outer part and the beading only with eggshell. Cut a piece of wallpaper to fit the panel and stick it down with wallpaper paste. When the paste has dried, apply a coat of water-based varnish so that the panel can be wiped clean.

flooring

Carpet is convenient in a nursery because it means your baby can play comfortably on the floor. However, the carpet will inevitably get stained, so don't buy an expensive one. Rather, invest in good-quality underlay and choose a man-made covering that is stain-resistant and can be scrubbed when necessary. Man-made fibres generate static and so are not ideal, but they are easier to clean. Choose a neutral colour and just accept that you will have to replace the carpet in a few years' time.

storage

Baskets are really excellent for storage because they are so flexible. Measure all the spaces where baskets could fit – under the bed, in wardrobes and on dressers – and take the measurements with you when you go shopping. You can buy baskets in all manner of sizes, shapes and styles, so you are bound to find something to suit. Matching, or contrasting, cotton liners are both practical and attractive (see pages 22–3 for instructions).

When using the baskets, do consider what you are putting where. Baskets that babies can reach should hold only things that you are happy for them to handle. Anything sharp or fragile must be stored well out of reach of tiny hands. Check the baskets themselves regularly as sharp wicker can cause nasty scratches. You don't have to throw the baskets away, just make sure they are out of reach.

Don't hide pretty clothes or toys away in wardrobes and cupboards. Instead, display them attractively to add colour and personality to the room. A gorgeous dress or cardigan on a lovely covered hanger looks sweet hanging from a hook or picture rail.

If you have limited storage space, hanging tidies that have different shaped and sized pockets are very useful, as are stacking boxes and crates. Remember that storage works only if it is easy to use.

◀ baskets galore
Matching baskets that slide under the cot or bed provide a good home for soft toys, and allow you to scoop them all up quickly and tuck them away at night.

finishing touches
Little things, such as pretty covered hangers and lavender sachets, make a difference in a well-designed nursery.

baby blue basket liner

Storage is an essential consideration in a baby's room and a wicker basket provides such a convenient and portable option that you will undoubtedly find a use for more than one. Lining the basket with a washable fabric not only makes it more attractive, but also avoids snagging baby items on the wicker.

you will need

- Rectangular storage basket
- Tape measure
- Fabric to fit the basket measurements
- Pins
- Sewing machine
- Sewing thread
- Elastic
- Safety pin

1 Measure the outside circumference of the basket and add 2cm (1in.) for seam allowances. Then take the internal height measurement, adding 10cm (4in.) for hems and the overlapping top edge. For the sides of the basket liner, cut one piece of fabric to these dimensions. Measure the internal width and length of the basket. For the base, cut one piece to these dimensions, allowing an extra 1cm (1/2in.) all round for the seam.

2 Right sides facing, pin and sew the short ends of the piece for the sides together to form a circle, taking a 1cm (1/2in.) seam allowance.

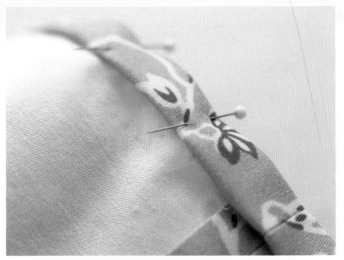

3 Turn over 1cm (1/2in.) around the top edge and then another 2.5cm (1in.) to make a casing. Sew close to the edge, leaving an opening for the elastic to be threaded through.

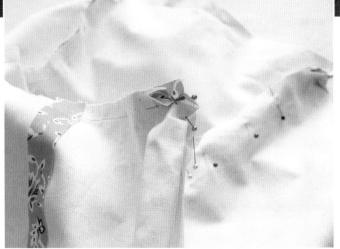

4 Right sides facing, sew the sides to the base of the liner, taking a 1cm (1/2in.) seam allowance, and making pleats at the corners so that the fabric fits neatly when it is in the basket.

5 Thread the elastic through the casing, using a safety pin. Sew the ends of the elastic together and sew up the opening. Turn the liner right side out and put it in the basket.

toys for the boys ... and girls
Babies don't differentiate between toys
for girls or boys, so there is no need for
you to do so. Just buy, or make, things
you like and think that your child will like.

play

This is such an important part of a child's development, as well as being fun for all concerned, that it needs to be designed into a nursery. We have discussed flooring (page 20), toys (page 17) and storage (page 21), and all of these things make important contributions to a child's activities. However, in order to let a tot develop her curiosity and skills to the full, it's worth considering the whole play environment.

Try to leave a decent-sized space in the room free of furniture and clutter so that your baby can roll and learn to crawl freely. Have a couple of toys on the floor (but where you won't stand on them), so that your baby can discover and retrieve them – finding your own playthings is always better than being handed something. If you are using basket storage (page 22), leave one basket of toys slightly pulled out so that your baby can investigate and pull out the things that take her fancy.

Designate an area of the house as the main play area – here it is the nursery – and try to keep toys in that space. Obviously, you will play with your baby in other rooms, but taking toys back to the play area at the end of the day will keep the rest of your home looking tidy and give you a visual respite once the baby has been put to bed.

comfort

Babies have sensitive skin and so proper laundering of all fabrics that they will come into contact with, not just their clothes, is essential. Bed linen and towels need to be washed in gentle detergent and well rinsed. Always make sure they are completely dry and aired before folding and storing them away.

finding fun
Babies are naturally curious and allowing your child to find her own playthings will stimulate her more than handing her toys to play with.

fresh approach
Keep clothes and linen fresh and sweet by airing and storing them properly.

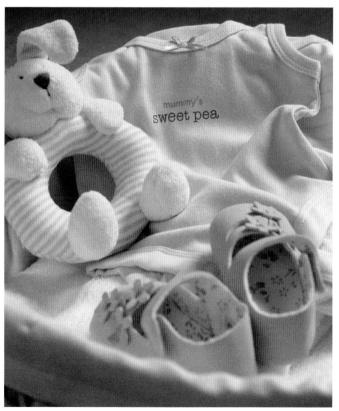

building blocks

Building blocks are always guaranteed playtime favourites and are so easy to make and decorate. These wooden blocks are the perfect educational toy and are sufficiently durable to last for years. Just make sure the blocks are not small enough for a curious baby to put in her mouth.

TIP Building blocks are classic toys for young children because they are simple and educational. Most children devise any number of games to play with them and each one helps to develop hand-eye co-ordination. What an achievement when the stack stays standing!

you will need

- A length of plain banister rail
- Saw
- Fine sandpaper
- Damp cloth
- PVA glue
- Water
- Paintbrush
- Car design on page 128
- Water-based acrylic varnish

1 Cut the blocks from the banister rail and sand the rough sides and edges until they feel smooth and silky to the touch.

2 Remove any dust with a damp cloth. Paint the cut sides with a solution of two parts PVA glue to one part water. Leave to dry.

3 Look at page 128 or choose your own designs to decorate the blocks. Photocopy them, preferably in colour, to fit your blocks and cut them out. You could use several colours and designs on each block.

4 To fix the designs to the blocks, use the PVA glue mixture as before. Leave each side of a block to dry before moving on to the next one – it won't take long. Once the blocks have been covered with designs, paint them with a water-based, waterproof varnish. Apply two coats, allowing them to dry in between.

vintage style

Wonderful vintage fabrics and wallpapers offer a way of creating a unique decorative scheme for a child's bedroom, full of personality and colour.

If, like so many creative people, you are a hoarder of fabrics, papers and *objets trouvés*, then you may well have all the materials you need to theme a room in vintage style. If not, hunting through second-hand shops, visiting auctions and jumble sales and investigating the many repro patterns and prints that are available should help you build up a treasure trove of lovely things. This decorative style allows you to combine and contrast all sorts of patterns and colours in the knowledge that you are adding to the final effect. However, there are some rules worth remembering, and sticking to. Choosing items from the same era and featuring at least some of the same colours will stop the room looking too chaotic, and using different-scale patterns allows the eye to focus on the various elements.

design

Children often have strong opinions about their room and what they want from it. Allowing them to express their creativity through the decoration of their space can teach you a lot about how they think and how they see their world. Encourage practical involvement by letting them decorate an item such as a toy chest, which they can then display in a prominent place.

personalizing

All children love seeing their name in lights, so to speak. Whether it is a wooden plaque on their bedroom door or a cross-stitch sampler over their bed, their own name has a powerful attraction. These appliquéd letter cushions (see pages 32–3 for instructions) are a fresh twist on the traditional lettered building blocks that generations of children have arranged to spell out their names. The vintage fabrics used for the letters are all of different patterns and, set against the plain cushion fronts, they sit harmoniously together. You need small amounts of these fabrics only, so recycling pieces from a much-loved but outgrown party dress, or the pretty but worn curtains that were previously in the room, will increase the sense of personalizing the space.

full of flowers
Using fabrics of different prints but all with a uniting theme can work beautifully, as these floral letters show.

back to back
Choose plainer fabrics for the cushion backs so that you can change the look of the room.

the room

There is quite a lot of furniture in this room, but that adds to the colourful, busy, vintage look. The tall, shelved storage unit, large chest of drawers and built-in wardrobe provide plenty of unobtrusive storage for books, toys and clothes. The wardrobe has double-height hanging rails, perfect for a small child's clothes.

The desk is positioned under the window so plenty of natural light is available for drawing and other craft activities.

Comfortable chairs offer seating for parents and child, essential if lulling your child off to sleep takes time, or if you are sitting up with her at night when she is ill.

The bed is full-size and so will last for years. This does mean that it takes up more space, but as it can be turned into a daybed, you do get value for space. Having the larger pieces of furniture around the edges of the room leaves the middle of it free for games and play on the floor.

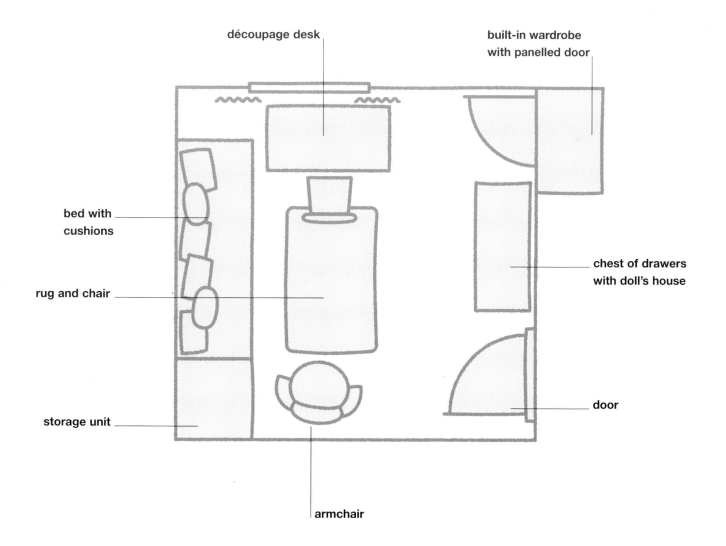

découpage desk

built-in wardrobe with panelled door

bed with cushions

rug and chair

chest of drawers with doll's house

storage unit

door

armchair

letter cushions

I've used scraps of vintage fabrics for the letters, off-white for the fronts and a selection of coloured ginghams and spots for the backs. Vintage buttons, or buttons covered with scraps of the letter fabrics, add a finishing touch, and the different shapes and sizes of the cushions provide an extra dimension. Brilliant for helping your child to spell her name, these cushions are reversible, so you can change the feel of the room in an instant.

You will need
- Letter cut out of paper
- Fusible webbing
- Pencil
- Iron
- Printed fabric large enough to fit the letter
- 33cm (13in.) square of natural cotton
- Sewing machine and sewing thread
- 33 x 25.5cm (13 x 10in.), 19 x 33cm (7½ x 13in.) and 11 x 3.5cm (4½ x 1½in.) pieces of printed fabric
- 30cm (12in.) square cushion pad
- Vintage and/or fabric-covered buttons

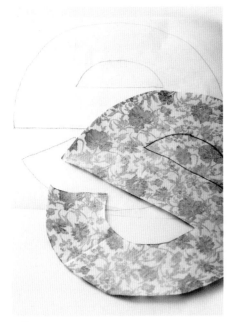

1 With the paper letter lying face down (so that it is back to front), lay the fusible webbing over it and trace off the outline onto the paper backing. Following the manufacturer's instructions, iron the webbing onto the back of the fabric and cut out the letter.

2 Peel the backing off the webbing and iron the letter onto the centre of the square of natural cotton. Set the sewing machine to a narrow satin stitch and stitch all around the letter.

3 Turn under and press a 2cm (¾in.) hem along one long edge of each of the two larger pieces of printed cotton. Press the long edges of the little strip of fabric to the middle, then press it in half lengthways.

4 Set the sewing machine to medium straight stitch and stitch down both long hems. Topstitch the strip of fabric close to the pressed edges. Fold the strip in half and sew it to the back of the hemmed edge of the smaller piece of printed fabric, positioning it centrally.

5 Right sides facing, pin the two pieces of printed cotton to the square of natural cotton, aligning the raw edges and making sure that the hemmed edge of the larger piece is lying over the edge with the loop. Machine-stitch around all four edges, taking a 1.5cm (½in.) seam allowance. Clip the corners, turn the cushion cover right side out and sew on a button to align with the loop. Insert the cushion pad.

double duty

This desk serves a two-fold function – it offers somewhere for your child to draw and paint and pursue other craft activities, and the drawer holds all manner of coloured pencils, pens, paper and other craft products ready for use. Buying or recycling a large desk means that it will also suit when your child is older and bigger.

longevity

When you are planning the room, consider for how long the scheme will be suitable. You will probably not want to redecorate in a year's time because your child is no longer happy with it. For this reason, think seriously if the latest 'must have' themes are what's wanted, and remember that characters from a television programme or game will quickly become outdated. If your child is really desperate to share his or her space with these characters, make them as temporary a feature as you can. For instance, make cushion covers in an inexpensive themed fabric so that they can be changed easily at a later date.

new from old

Vintage style allows you to incorporate items from your own childhood, or even your parents' childhoods, into a room. Refurbishing a desk or chest of drawers can transform it into a fresh piece that perfectly suits the new décor. A crocheted blanket that you snuggled up in makes a brilliant bedcover for a child's first 'grown-up' bed. Choose a plain duvet cover and valance to keep the emphasis on the bedspread. Covers and cushions allow the bed to be changed into a sofa, perfect when lots of friends visit.

Simple sill-length, pinch-pleat curtains can be made from larger curtains cut down to the new size. Launder the fabric before cutting it and line the curtains with crisp new cotton lining fabric. On a practical note, always make sure that the curtain pole above the window is wide enough to allow the curtains to be drawn back completely to let as much natural light as possible into the room.

Old lampshades can be re-covered with fabric (see pages 108–9 for instructions), either by you or by a specialist company. This offers another way to co-ordinate the design scheme down to the last detail.

design and detail
Tiny elements, such as the vintage and fabric-covered buttons on the cushion backs, can help make a design scheme cohesive.

découpage table

I've used a blank piece of children's furniture that can be painted to suit the room. To découpage the table I've used one piece of wrapping paper: cutting out the motifs didn't take too long. Then comes the fun part – working out where you're going to place them. Here, less is most definitely more. You want some motifs on show on the table top but the rest need to be a bit harder to find – maybe a few in the drawer or down the sides of the desk. The design on the top should be understated because the top will get filled up with the little essentials that girls love – trinkets, jewellery, hairbrushes and clips.

You will need
- Desk or table
- Paintbrush and small varnish roller
- Water-based primer
- Water-based eggshell paint
- Wrapping paper with printed motifs
- Small, sharp scissors
- Sheet of rough paper
- Small paintbrush
- PVA adhesive
- Water-based satin varnish

1 Using the brush or roller, whichever is appropriate to the part of the table you are treating, prime and then paint the table twice. Each time, leave to dry completely. This may take a couple of days.

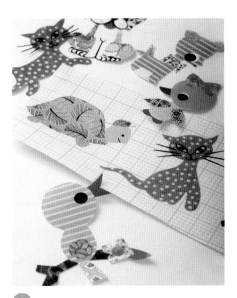

2 Cut out motifs from the wrapping paper with the scissors. Make sure you cut them out neatly to give a really professional finish.

3 Arrange the motifs on the painted table. When you are happy with the arrangement, you are ready to glue them in place.

4 Lay the motifs on some rough paper and use the small paintbrush to brush a thin layer of undiluted PVA over the back of each one. Do not allow glue to touch the surface of the motifs while brushing it on the back, because it can mark them. Position each motif on the desk and smooth it down. If glue squeezes out from under a motif, wipe it away with a lightly dampened cloth. Leave to dry.

5 Using the small paintbrush, brush varnish over each motif. Leave to dry.

large toys

Doll's houses, forts, play kitchens and similar large toys all take up valuable space in a child's bedroom, so it can be tempting to dismiss them as 'a waste of space'. However, they can be an integral feature and, if chosen carefully in consultation with your child, will provide hours and hours of playing fun, making them excellent 'value for space'. Encourage the child to see the toy as a work in progress rather than a final result and to make new pieces for it, such as doll's bedding and curtains from fabric scraps or hand-drawn pictures, framed with lolly sticks, for the walls.

made with love
Use scraps of decorating fabrics to make soft toys that suit the design scheme as well as being fun to play with.

framed notice board

An old gilded picture frame that had seen better days was the starting point for this magnetic notice board. Recycling items in this way is rewarding, as well as cost-effective. A sheet of steel covered in lightweight ticking allows your children to use magnets to display their artworks and photographs – much safer than pins. Don't use thick fabric to cover the steel because the magnets won't cling properly.

You will need
- Picture frame
- Sandpaper
- Water-based primer and eggshell paint
- Paintbrush
- Metal spreader
- Impact adhesive
- Square of galvanized steel to fit in picture frame
- Square of fabric 5cm (2in.) larger than the steel all around
- Panel pins
- Hammer
- Badge and magnet kits
- Scraps of fabric and ribbon

1 Make sure that the frame is clean and sand off any loose paint. Prime before painting, if it is a dark colour it may require a couple of coats of primer. Two thin coats are more effective than one thick coat. Leave to dry then paint the frame.

2 Use the spreader to spread a thin layer of impact adhesive across the steel. Lay the square of fabric centrally on the adhesive and smooth it down. Fold the edges of the fabric over the steel and glue them to the back. I've covered the back with the same fabric, to disguise the turned-over edges, because I do like the back of things to look as nice as the front. This is optional.

3 Fit the fabric-covered steel panel into the painted frame, holding it in place with panel pins.

4 Make up a series of decorative magnets using the kits and scraps of vintage fabrics and ribbon.

eco nursery

Bringing a new baby into the world focuses attention on the environment they will grow up in. Ecologically aware nursery design can be beneficial now and in the future.

Creating a room for a new baby is exciting but can also be a little daunting, and you may feel that the task is enough in itself without having to worry about the environment as well. However, there are ways of contributing to the green movement through good design, and your room can be both beautiful and ecologically sound. Start by planning the space carefully; making mistakes and then having to buy replacement items is expensive in more ways than one.

colour

Choose colours that aren't too babyish, so that the room won't date, and create a nursery atmosphere with well-chosen accessories. Soft tones of white and cream make for a very tranquil space, and if you don't know whether you are having a boy or a girl, they are perfectly appropriate for either. The nursery should be a place for sleeping and relaxing, so avoid using bright colours – there are times when stimulation is a good thing for babies, but not when you are trying to lay them down for a sleep. There are various eco-friendly paints you can choose from (see Suppliers, page 136) and they come in wonderful, calming colours.

the room

The first step in planning your nursery is to keep things simple, especially if the room is quite small. You really don't need that much equipment at first and you can always buy more as you find that you do need it.

A bed with a good mattress is a must, and there are plenty to choose from that are both natural in origin and healthy for your baby. A bed can be made enchanting with muslin draped around it, acting as soft curtains. Another must is a comfortable armchair – for you rather than the baby.

A capacious chest of drawers will hold a surprising number of clothes and other necessaries, and can be supplemented with a wardrobe painted to match when the child is older.

Trimming a rug (see pages 50–2 for instructions) is another way of recycling a piece of soft furnishing to co-ordinate with the newly decorated room.

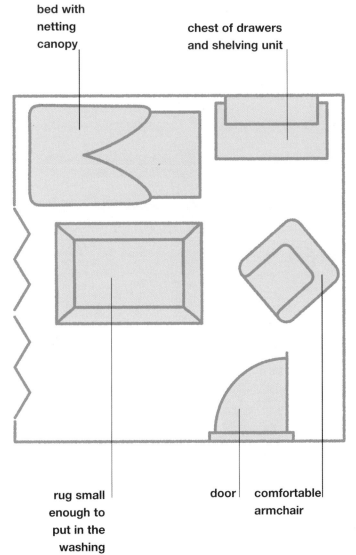

bed with netting canopy

chest of drawers and shelving unit

rug small enough to put in the washing machine

door

comfortable armchair

craft skills
Don't be afraid. The least creative of us can use simple stamping and painting techniques to personalize a room. These tags were made for the keepsake frames opposite and on page 46.

furniture

While you will have to buy some new things, opportunities will arise with this style of nursery for refurbishing and reusing older pieces of furniture. Items that might look heavy, old-fashioned or tired can look completely different given a fresh coat of pastel paint and a set of new handles. Chests of drawers and wardrobes, for instance, just need cleaning and repainting to take on new life as nursery furniture. Look in second-hand shops, and at auctions, and try to see items on offer in a new light. A hallway coat rack, for example, makes a great display and hanging unit for your baby's room.

paint perfect

Take time to clean old furniture thoroughly before repainting. Sand any rough areas and fill any holes or knocks before painting with a water-based eggshell paint.

keepsake frame

Create a series of sweetly sentimental pictures by framing
memorabilia, such as photographs, tiny toys, baby shoes and
a note about your baby's first steps, tied with ribbon. Layering
smaller items and adding labels and cut-outs will make the most
of your items and create keepsakes that you and your child
will treasure. You could even add a sealed letter, to be opened
in years to come, telling of your feelings for your little one.

You will need

- Box frame with mount
- Metal spreader
- Impact adhesive
- Square of fabric the size of the back
  of the frame
- Smaller squares of fabric with frayed edges
- Glass-headed pin and decorated tag
- Square of printed paper
- Photograph
- Decorative paperclip
- Glue dots
- Button heart motif

1 Dismantle the box frame. Use the
spreader to spread a thin layer of impact
adhesive across the back panel. Lay the
square of fabric on the adhesive and
smooth it down.

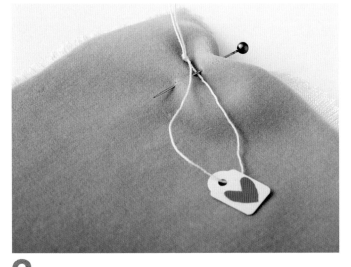

2 Lay two frayed squares on top of one another and pin the
decorated tag to them.

3 Assemble squares of fabric, paper and the photograph and
hold them together with the paperclip. Use impact adhesive to
stick the montage to the background.

4 Use glue dots to stick the button heart motif to the front of the montage.

5 Leave the glue to dry completely overnight, and then reassemble the frame, placing the mount up against the glass.

sleep

You will obviously need a bed for your baby, and there are various options to choose from. A cot bed can be a great investment as it is usually suitable for a child up to five years old and some of them are very attractively designed and made. Look for furniture made from sustainable sources. A new baby can look a little lost in such a big space, but you can buy special barriers to fit inside larger cots that make the sleeping space smaller for little babies. Alternatively, for the first few months, when the baby will probably be sleeping in your room, a cot with an adjustable mattress height is a good idea.

Some beautiful baby mattresses are available, made from natural and organic materials that are breathable, non-allergenic, chemical-free and naturally fire-retardant. Bamboo and organic cotton bed linen is also worth considering. Easily washable and gorgeously soft and silky to the touch, fabric made from bamboo is also environmentally friendly, since the plants thrive without pesticides and, unlike cotton, with relatively little water.

light

A nursery with natural light flooding in is lovely, but do be sure that your baby is not sleeping in direct sunlight. This really can be dangerous because babies can overheat very quickly. If the cot is to be near a window, invest in, or make, blackout curtains, which are lined to block the light. Wooden shutters with adjustable louvres are another good option, although they can be more expensive.

Choose low-energy lightbulbs for the lamps in the room, and if you are going to have a nightlight, consider a plug-in one that uses very little power. All of the small actions you take to reduce your carbon footprint are well worth the minimal effort involved.

natural fabrics
Soft furnishings, including bedding, made from natural fibres are pleasanter to touch, and more environmentally friendly, than those composed of man-made fibres. But beware of wool fabrics because they can be itchy to a baby's sensitive skin.

mat with fabric border

Customise a recycled rug to co-ordinate perfectly with your child's room.
If the rug has thick hems, cut them off or unpick them so that the edges fit
under your sewing machine. Remember to think practically and don't use
anything too big, or it won't go in the washing machine. Wash your chosen
fabric and rug separately before adding the fabric borders, especially if the
colours are strong. Once you have mastered this project, you can add
decorative borders to blankets and bedcovers in the same way.

You will need
- Cotton mat
- Four strips of cotton fabric, each measuring 25cm (10in.) wide by the length of one side of the rug plus 25cm (10in.)
- Iron
- Scissors
- Sewing machine and sewing thread
- Hand-sewing needle

1 Press the strips in half lengthways. Fold over the corners at each end and press. Cut along the pressed diagonal lines to remove the triangles of fabric.

2 Open the strips out flat. Right sides facing, pin the pointed ends of two adjacent strips together. Machine stitch the points together, stopping and starting the stitching 1.5cm (½in.) in from the edge of the fabric. This will make attaching the fabric edge easier. Stitch all the strips together in this way to form a square. Press under a 1.5cm (½in.) seam allowance all around one edge of the square.

3 Right sides facing and aligning the edges, pin the raw edge of the fabric square to the edges of the mat. Machine stitch along the edges, taking a 1.5cm (1/2in.) seam allowance.

4 Snip the tips off the fabric points. Turn the fabric right side out, folding it along the original lengthways pressed lines so that the pressed-under edge is lying against the back of the mat. Press all the mitre seams open and the corners flat.

5 Using the needle and thread, slip-stitch the pressed edge of the fabric border to the back of the mat.

make and match
Making simple soft furnishings allows you to co-ordinate the room perfectly at relatively little cost.

sensitive skin
Wash all baby items, toys included, in gentle detergent, and where possible use washing balls and dryer balls to save energy.

washing

Everything you provide for your baby in the way of soft furnishings, clothes and toys should be capable of being washed in the washing machine, ideally at a low temperature. From an eco perspective, you should also think about reusable nappies. These are kinder to the environment than disposables, less expensive, and many parents believe they make the toilet-training process easier and faster. However, they do need laundering and if you don't want to use a tumble dryer, this can mean nappies draped around the house throughout the winter. A nappy laundering service may be the answer.

slot-together toy

Learning to build is a very important part of growing up and these

big slot-together pieces will allow children to build their own den.

The soft colours I've used work well in this room, but you could add

patterns, animals or letters of the alphabet to help with reading.

I recommend having the pieces cut professionally so that they are

perfectly square. I've been careful to use child-friendly paints only

throughout this book. The colours are brilliant and I've been very

pleasantly surprised at how good the paints are.

You will need

- 25 30cm (12in.) squares of 3mm MDF
- Protective face mask
- Pencil and ruler
- G-clamps
- Drill with 5mm bit
- Tenon saw
- Sandpaper
- Small paintbrush
- Small varnish roller
- Paint tray
- Water-based primer
- Water-based eggshell paints

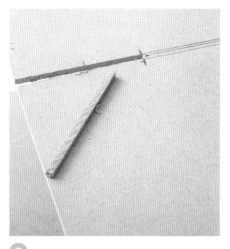

1 Measure and mark the centre point of one side of a square. Measure 8cm (3in.) in from the mark and make a second mark. Lay the edge of another square between the two marks and draw around it. The resulting drawn rectangle must lie at right angles to the edge of the square.

2 Using G-clamps, clamp the square to a work surface. Drill a hole at the inner end of the drawn rectangle. Use the protective face mask when drilling and sawing.

3 Using the tenon saw, cut along the drawn lines up to the drilled hole. This will cut out a thin strip of MDF. Repeat steps 1–3 on each edge of the square. Check the diagram on page 129 if you are unsure of where to drill and cut.

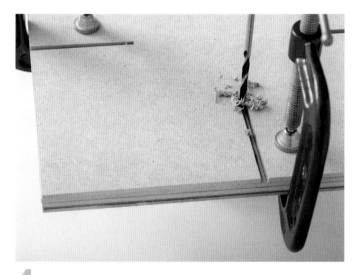

4 Lay the slotted square on top of three blank ones and clamp all four together with the G-clamps. Using the top square as a template, drill and cut all the slots in the three blank squares. Repeat steps 1–4 until all the squares are slotted.

5 Sand the edges of the MDF and wipe off dust. Using the paintbrush, prime the insides of the slots, brushing out any drips that appear on the other side. Using the roller, prime one side of each square. Leave to dry vertically, then turn them over and prime the other sides. In the same way, paint all the squares with two coats of eggshell. Leave them standing upright to dry for a week so that the paint is fully hardened, not just touch dry.

outdoor den

Children need their own space where they can play and use their imaginations, and a den is the perfect answer. We all made camps from up-turned chairs and blankets when we were small and having a specially designed den must be every child's dream.

If you have a garden and can devote a small section of it to making a play area, a 2 x 3 metre (6 x 8ft) garden shed is a great starting point for a superb den. If space is a problem, then consider a collapsible wigwam or playhouse that can be put up and taken down as need be. The advantage of a permanent den is, of course, that a lot of the children's clutter can live in it, rather than filling up the house. Obviously, a den will get more use in the summer than in the winter, particularly if it isn't heated, but even in cold weather it will provide great storage for larger play items.

decorating a den

Keep decoration simple and inexpensive, as most of the colour, styling and detailing will come from the children's possessions. Paint the inside walls, ceiling and floor plain white for maximum light and a fresh look. If the budget can stretch to it, buy a piece of man-made fibre carpet or a piece of lino to cover the floor – proper flooring goes a long way towards transforming a humble shed into a cosy den. If the den has windows, simple cotton curtains can be quickly run up on the sewing machine and will help make the space feel like a real room.

clutter-free home
Make a deal with the children that in return for having their own space, they keep their larger playthings in it.

the room

This den is large enough to hold everything two active young boys need to keep themselves occupied. So, although it is a more expensive option than a small shed, it repays the investment in that you don't have to listen to drum practice!

Careful planning will make the most of the available space. As with all children's rooms, keep the storage simple and practical. For instance, a cotton tidy with generous pockets can hang on the wall, taking up little space but providing lots of storage. The collection shelf (see pages 64–5 for instructions) offers a home to all manner of found and treasured tiny objects. Put up hooks, Shaker-style peg rails and solid shelving, all of which help to keep floor space free.

A desk and chairs offer seating, and a rug is for sprawling on while discussing football with friends. A sleeping shelf has been built into the roof space of this den, accessed by the step ladder, offering a space for a quiet afternoon nap.

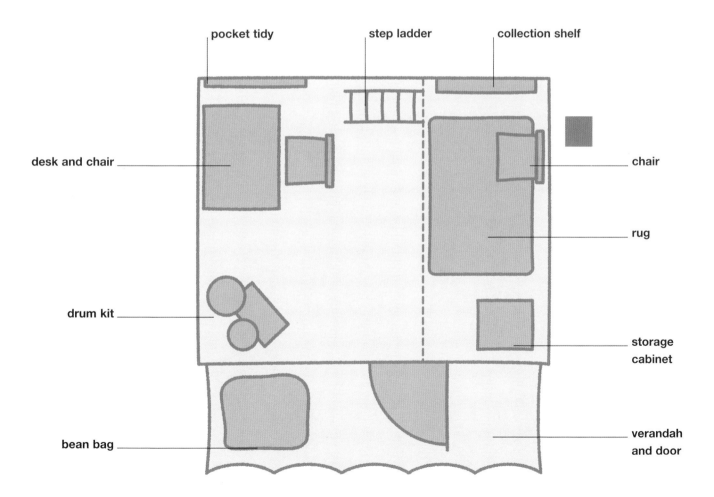

fabric and photo bunting

Give classic bunting a fresh twist by personalizing it with photographs. The photos were sent by email to a printing company (see Suppliers, page 136) who printed them onto white fabric and posted them back – so simple. Colourful plains, stripes and motif fabrics were used to make other flags.

You will need
- Template on page 128
- Paper
- Scissors
- Fabrics cut to 44 x 19cm (17 x 8in.) strips
- Pins
- Pinking shears
- Sewing machine and thread
- Thin cord or bias binding
- Bodkin

1 Enlarge the template to the desired size (here, it measures 21cm (8in.) from top to bottom) and cut out a paper pattern. Fold a strip of fabric in half widthways and pin the pattern to it with the straight top edge against the fold.

2 Using the pinking shears, cut out the fabric flag.

3 Machine-stitch across the top of the flag, 1.5cm (¹/₂in.) from the folded edge, to make a channel for the cord.

4 If you are using bias binding, fold it in half and machine-stitch close to the edge to make a narrow cord. Using the bodkin, thread the flags onto the cord to make the bunting.

storage

This will depend on the size and structure of the den, but remember that unless it's easy to use, you might as well not bother to have any at all because it won't get used. In any case, the den is bound to become almost instantly untidy as soon as the children start playing in it, but that will be part of their fun. Make an agreement with them that it should be tidied up, more or less, at the end of the day and properly tidied up every week or so. Ask them what storage they need to keep their den tidy and then they will have no excuse for not using it!

If your children love to draw, put up a sturdy cord around the top of the den walls and give them a supply of clothes pegs. They can use these to peg up their masterpieces and create their own gallery – and keep their drawings and paintings tidy at the same time.

fabrics and colour

Keep the colour scheme bright and fresh with white paint and splashes of primary colours. Since this den is used by two boys, checks and ticking stripes in reds and blues are very suitable, with a small number of cowboy and racing-car prints. If you are decorating a den for girls, you could use spotty fabrics and multi-coloured stripes for a more girly feel and add pattern with bold floral prints. Whatever you choose, in a small space such as this keep the colour palette simple. From a practical point of view, make sure that all the fabrics are washable, because they will get grubby pretty quickly.

The rug in this den (pictured on page 58) was specially made using one of the children's artworks as a design. You simply send off the drawing (see Suppliers page 136) and the finished rug arrives back in the post! It's an amazing way to personalize your child's space.

mix and match
If you keep to a limited colour palette (here it's red, white and blue), you can combine different patterns without making the space feel chaotic.

◀ put out more flags
Bunting is an inexpensive and quick way to add colour and cheery style to a playroom. They need just small amounts of fabric, so you could use scraps, as here, or even consider recycling old clothes to make them.

collection shelf

Children are often avid collectors, so make a special shelf where they can display their collections of little toys, treasures such as shells and feathers found on walks, and favourite marbles. From a practical point of view, a collection shelf stops these items spreading everywhere and getting vacuumed up – always a cause for tears. Save attractive glass jars for your shelf, but make sure the opening is big enough for a child to put a hand in without its getting stuck!

You will need
- Shelf
- Ruler
- Pencil
- Bradawl
- Glass jars with metal lids
- Drill and drill bit
- Safety goggles
- Screwdriver
- Screws shorter than the thickness of the shelf

1 Turn the shelf upside down, measure and mark the middle at several points across its width. Using the marks as a guide, draw a line along its length. Then, by measuring or by eye, mark where each jar will be positioned along this line.

2 On the underside of each lid, mark the centre with a bradawl.

3 Draw a line across the underside of the lid through the centre mark you have made. Make two more marks, equally spaced, either side of the centre mark. Wearing safety goggles, drill holes in the lid at the marked points.

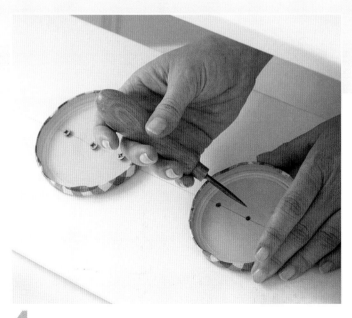

4 Position the lid with the holes aligned with the line drawn along the shelf. Push the tip of the bradawl through each hole in the lid to make a guide hole in the shelf.

5 Using the screwdriver, drive a screw through each drilled hole, securing the lid to the underside of the shelf. Screw a jam jar onto each lid.

bean bag

This is a must for watching television, reading and playing.

Why not create a series of bean bags for a den or playroom,

using different fabrics? Mix stripes with checks, and bold prints

with colourful plain fabrics, for a vibrant scheme. In this design,

the cover is easily removed, and making it in washable fabrics

ensures easy cleaning.

You will need

- Two 123 x 93cm (48 x 37in.) pieces of curtain lining or calico
- Sewing machine and thread
- Polystyrene beans
- Cereal box

- Two 123 x 93cm (48 x 37in.) pieces of fabric plus a 28 x 11.5cm (11 x 4¹/₂in.) strip of fabric for handle
- 93cm (37in.) of sew-on hook-and-loop tape

1 Right sides facing, machine stitch the pieces of curtain lining together around all the edges, taking a 1.5cm (¹/₂in.) seam allowance, and leaving a gap in one end. Turn 14cm (5¹/₂in.) right side out. Fill the bag three-quarters full with beans through a cardboard cone made from the cereal box. (Beans don't seem to stick to the box.) Machine stitch the opening closed.

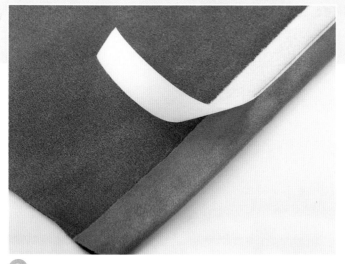

2 Press under a 2.5cm (1in.) hem on one short edge of each of the large pieces of fabric. Machine-stitch one side of the hook-and-loop tape to each hem, covering the raw edges of the fabric.

3 Right sides facing, pin the two large pieces of fabric together and machine stitch around the three raw edges, taking a 1.5cm (¹/₂in.)seam allowance. Turn the cover right side out and press seams.

4 Press the strip of fabric (for the handle) in half lengthways, right sides facing. Taking a 1.5cm (½in.) seam allowance, stitch along the long edge. Turn right side out and press flat. Press under 1.5cm (½in.) at each short end.

5 Machine stitch a line 5cm (2in.) in from the edge around all three seamed sides to form a flange. Centre the handle on the flange on the opposite end to the hook-and-loop tape. Machine stitch across the ends of the handle. Put the filled liner into the cover and press the hook-and-loop tape closed.

room to grow

As children mature their tastes change, so plan a room that will not only suit them now, but can be adapted to suit them just as well as they get older.

Once your child has grown out of the nursery, think carefully about how to change the room so that the basic décor will last for several years. This is an especially good idea when it comes to buying bedroom furniture, which can be expensive. It is better for your finances – and for the planet – to buy well-made pieces that will survive for a good while than to purchase inexpensive but cheaply made pieces that will quickly need replacing. Keeping the walls and floors of the room fairly neutral and investing in good-quality, adult-sized furniture will allow you to make small alterations to change the look of the room without completely redecorating and refurnishing.

themes

Choosing an overall specific theme for a room can help formulate and concentrate ideas, but beware of choosing something that your child will tire of quickly, no matter how much he may like it right now. The best bet is to make sure the themed elements of the room are either removable, or easily and inexpensively replaceable. In this boy's room, for instance, the spaceman theme is confined to posters, pictures and cotton bed linen (see pages 72–3 for instructions).

the room

When you are planning a room to last, take as many elements into account as possible. Choose furniture that can be moved around rather than built-in pieces, and concentrate on the right sort of storage – there is no point in having lots of bookshelves if your child isn't a natural reader and prefers spending leisure time making models.

The adult-sized wardrobe easily accommodates all the child's clothes and can be complemented with a matching chest of drawers in the future if need be. The high-level bed not only appeals to a child's climbing instinct but also has storage space underneath. At the moment this space is used as part of the general play area, but later a chest of drawers or low-level cupboards could go there.

Banner curtains (see pages 80–81 for instructions) provide colour at little cost, and a big rug helps to soften the look and soundproof the wooden floor.

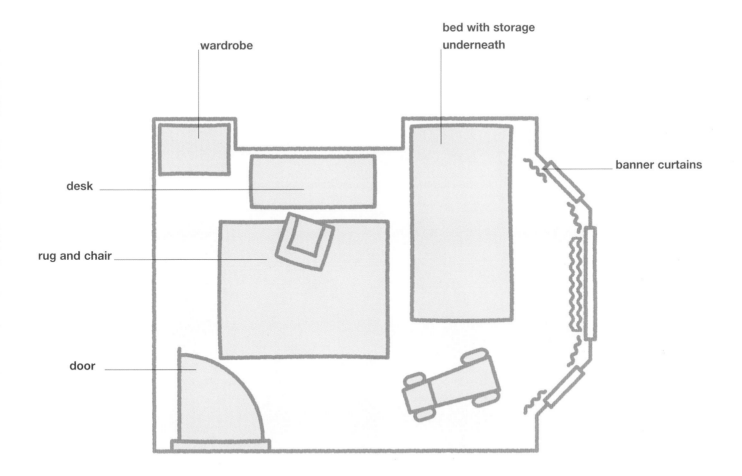

wardrobe

bed with storage underneath

banner curtains

desk

rug and chair

door

spaceman bed linen

Simple stencilling allows you to create bed linen that co-ordinates perfectly with your child's room, but doesn't cost the earth. Pick colours used elsewhere in the room and a stencil motif that suits the design scheme.

You will need

- Duvet cover
- Machine fabric dye
- Salt
- Brown paper
- Spaceman stencil in three layers
- Low-tack spray glue
- Stencil brush
- Fabric paints

There are many different stencils available from various sources (see Suppliers page 136) so you are sure to find something to suit your child's room. Whether it be pretty flowers for a little girl's nursery or abstract geometrics for a boy's room, you can use stencils to add design and detail to the space easily and quickly.

1 If it is new, wash the duvet cover to remove any fabric finishing. Then dye it using machine fabric dye, and salt to fix the colour, following the manufacturer's instructions. Dry the duvet cover and iron it before stencilling.

2 Lay a piece of brown paper inside the duvet cover, just in case some of the paint leaks through the top layer. Spray the back of the stencil with glue and position it on the front of the duvet cover. Dab a small amount of fabric paint on to the stencil brush and, using a stabbing motion, apply the paint through the stencil. Leave to dry.

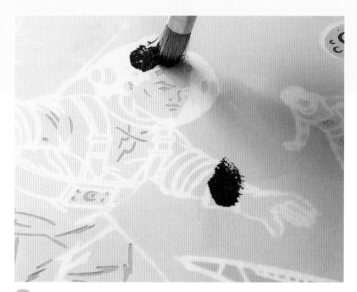

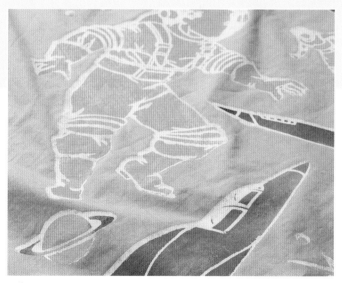

3 When using a three-part stencil, it is important to use the reference dots on each corner so that each layer of the stencil lines up perfectly. Stencil the second layer in the same way as the first and leave to dry. Try using more than one colour of paint, graduating it as you dab the paint on to the fabric.

4 Finally, line up the third layer of the stencil and stencil in the details in a strong colour so that they show up well.

super storage
Make storage flexible – wide, deep shelves will hold books of all sizes as well as other toys and display pieces.

divided up
Drawers with dividers, either built in or purchased separately, are a great idea. They prevent the drawer from becoming one huge mess of clutter and help in continuing efforts towards tidiness.

clutter

Most children are untidy. They have relatively short attention spans and move from one game to another, leaving the last plaything wherever it may lie. They also like to have their possessions around them, so that they can see everything in their little kingdom. As long as they keep their things confined to their room, it's not a bad idea to indulge them. Make a deal that the room will get tidied up once a week or so, enough to vacuum and do basic cleaning, but other than that, let clutter accumulate. Once or twice a year have a big clean (before Christmas, say, which tends to bring a new haul of possessions), and filter out some of the discarded items.

creativity

Giving children the space to be both physically and mentally creative is an important part of their development. Whether they want to paint, read, build fantastic structures from Lego or make their own toy aeroplanes, if they can do this in their own room, so much the better – for them and for the rest of your home!

Keeping the floor as clear of furniture as possible allows space for ongoing projects. However, a desk is useful for smaller pieces and for the inevitable homework to come, and its drawers provide useful storage space. Although miniature chests and cupboards take up more room, they do provide somewhere safe to keep all sorts of small but precious items.

kids will be kids
Painted floorboards are a good option in an active child's room. Spills can easily be cleaned up and when the floor eventually gets too scratched, it can be repainted.

storage case

Vintage suitcases make great storage, stylishly hiding away treasures of all shapes and sizes. Covering the inside with a paper collage personalizes the project and adds a splash of colour. Try using comics, your child's own drawings, or even old textbooks for the academically inclined!

You will need
- An old suitcase or trunk
- Leather balm, to clean up the leather
- Cloth
- Comics, wrapping paper, cards, old textbooks or any other suitable paper
- PVA glue and water
- Paintbrush
- Water-based acrylic varnish

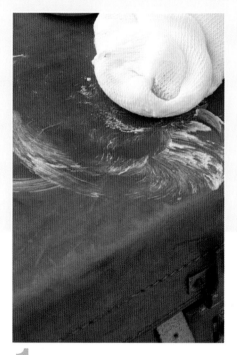

1 Clean and condition the suitcase with an appropriate cleaner or balm.

2 Tear up pieces of the coloured paper. If you tear with the front facing you, the paper will have a white edge and if you tear with the back facing you, it won't. Try both techniques to see which look you prefer.

3 Dilute two parts of PVA glue with one part water to make a solution. Using the paintbrush, brush the solution over the back of the torn paper, then stick the pieces to the inside of the case. In order to smooth out any air bubbles, you may have to lift the paper up and down a few times so it's taut. Overlap the edges so that the inside is completely covered. Leave to dry.

The same technique can be used to refurbish all sorts of storage items and pieces of furniture. Try covering the insides of cabin trunks or plain MDF cupboards, both of which are great for children's rooms. If you love this look, extend it and use it to cover the outsides of pieces of furniture as well. A shabby wardrobe can be given a new lease of life with a colourful covering that conceals any scrapes and dents.

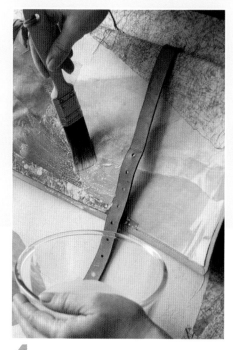

4 Paint a coat of varnish over the paper to protect it.

storage

The three Ss – storage, storage, storage – are an especially vital part of any older child's room (boring but true). Including good freestanding or built-in storage really will help you and your child manage the space efficiently.

A good way to approach planning for this is to write down a list of everything that needs to be stored. Note literally everything – from toys to socks, to school books, to sports kit and skateboards. Whatever the items are, plan for them – don't pretend they are not there just because you don't like them.

Then think about what kind of storage you need for each item – write it down on the list next to each one with some idea of how much space is needed. Then add 10 per cent (at least) to the requirements to allow room for the accumulation of more things. Put all the storage ideas together and you should come up with the amount and type of furniture you need to provide. This type of careful planning should mean that everything has a home and so, if the mood takes him, your child can quite easily and quickly tidy the room.

toy time
Toys aren't just for playing with and then putting away – they can be part of the decoration of the room. Provide display space and encourage your child to use it.

flexible space

Above all, in a room that you hope to adapt as your child grows, the more flexible the space can be, the better. Hence the necessity of choosing freestanding furniture rather than built-in pieces, where possible, so that it can be moved around the room. An alcove that now holds a wardrobe may one day be a great nook for a computer table, while the wardrobe might move to stand against a wall alongside a matching chest of drawers.

◀ we come in peace
Huge posters and canvas prints are an obvious and eye-catching way of creating an easily changeable theme for a room.

banner curtains

Curtains for a large window can be expensive and time-consuming to make. Dress curtains, which are not meant to close but simply add a touch of softness and colour to the room, are the answer here, in combination with a blind. I have used four different fabric designs to form vertical strips of bold colour in the corners of the window, unified by the plain band across the top.

You will need

- Fabric the desired width of the curtain plus 4cm (1¹/₂in.) by the length minus 25cm (10in.)
- Contrasting fabric the desired width of the curtain by 27cm (11in.)
- Pins
- Sewing machine and thread
- Tape measure
- Heading tape
- Curtain hooks

1 Right sides facing, pin the contrast fabric to the top of the main fabric and, taking a 1.5cm ($^1/_2$in.) seam allowance, machine stitch the pieces together. Press the seam allowance to the top and top stitch 1cm ($^3/_8$in.) up from the seam.

2 Turn under a double 1cm ($^1/_2$in.) hem along the side and bottom edges and stitch in place.

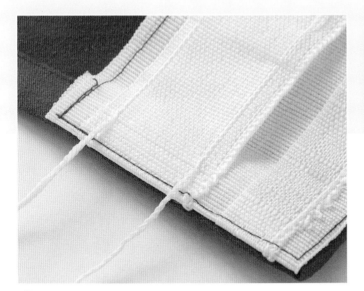

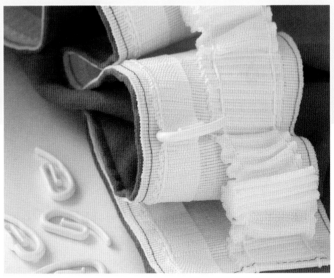

3 Cut the heading tape to the width of the curtain plus 4cm (1$^1/_2$in.), then pull the cords out at one end and knot them. Turn under 1.5cm ($^1/_2$in.) along the top edge of the curtain. Pin the tape across the top of the curtain, folding under 2cm ($^3/_4$in.) at each end. At one end, keep the knotted cords free; at the other end, turn them under so that they will be stitched in place. Stitch right around the tape, close to the edges.

4 Pull the free ends of the cords to gather up the tape. Tie the cords together but do not cut off the ends. Slip the curtain hooks into the loops on the back.

nursery colour

Wonderful colours and fabrics can be used in a child's room to match the adults' rooms in the house. You may need to make some concessions, but remember that the nursery is a room for you as well as your child and you should both be happy there.

Creating a nursery that is suitable for a little girl or boy, and at the same time echoes the rest of the house, will make it a comfortable space for your child and for you. This is important since you will undoubtedly be spending a great deal of time in the room. Some ideas and design schemes don't easily translate into children's rooms – for example, the modern minimal look can be very hard to maintain – but others that rely on colour and pattern just need a little thought and a few compromises.

colour

All-over, vibrant colour is not a good idea in a nursery, where it's better if a calmer atmosphere prevails, but it can be introduced in bright accents against pastel-coloured walls. The lovely green walls in this room provide a pleasing backdrop for the colourful mural (see pages 94–5 for instructions) and hot-pink curtains.

Just because a room is for a little girl, as this one is, doesn't mean it has to be pink. Pick a shade of a colour that sits happily with pink so that you can introduce elements of that if you or your little girl wish.

wall style
A large-scale wallpaper mural is a good way to bring splashes of rich, bold colour into an otherwise gentle room.

the room

This is a very simple room, containing the absolute minimum of furniture and relying on colour and pattern for the principal decoration. As the child grows up and acquires more possessions, more items, such as a chest of drawers, can be introduced.

A big, colourful, butterfly-shaped rug occupies the middle of the room and the cot stands against the wall opposite the mural. This gives the child a great view of the jungle patterns.

An old chair with a fresh slip cover (see pages 90–91 for instructions) occupies one corner, giving parents a place to sit, while scatter cushions and a bean bag provide plenty of comfortable floor-level seating for the child.

The two big wardrobes are built into the alcoves either side of the cot, which, as it is oval, does not block access to them. The wardrobes are fitted out with rails and shelves to hold both clothes and toys.

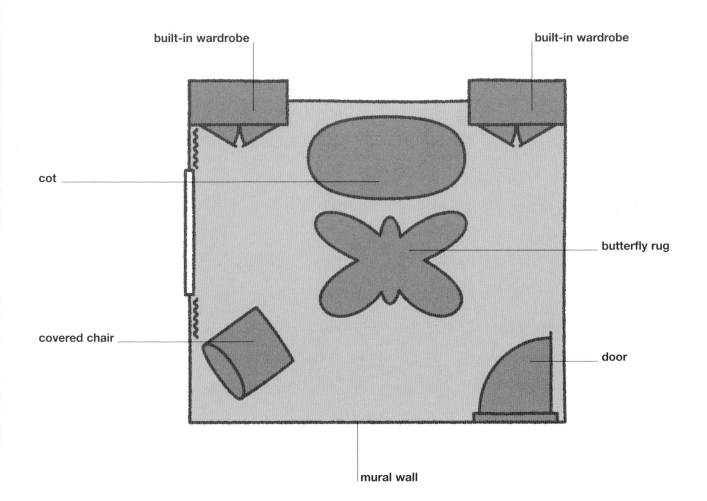

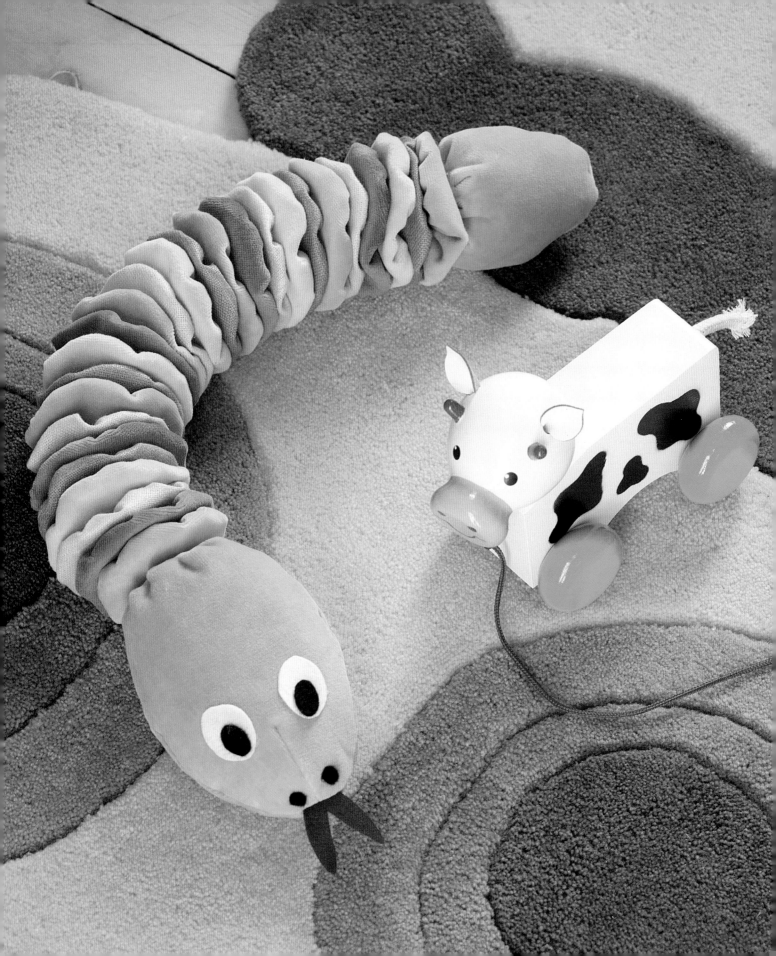

stretchy snake

A fresh twist on a traditional toy, this retro snake will charm all little children. It's simple to make and, of course, the choice of colours is up to you. You just need some scraps of fabrics – I've used the softest cotton velvet and a cotton-and-linen mix fabric – to create a really tactile friend to keep your child company at night.

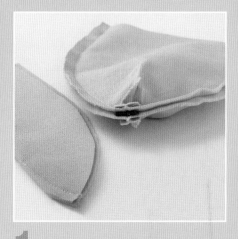

You will need

- Templates on page 130
- Two heads, two tails and two 7cm (3in.) circles all in the same fabric
- Tongue cut from red felt
- Sewing machine and sewing thread
- Scissors
- Washable toy stuffing
- 1.5m (1³⁄₄yd.) of cord elastic and bodkin
- 15cm (6in.) circles of fraying fabrics
- 14cm (5¹⁄₂in.) circles of non-fraying fabrics (how many depends on how long you want the snake to be)
- Eyes and nostrils cut from white and black felt; fabric glue
- Bell (optional)

1 Machine-stitch the dart in both head pieces. Pin the tongue to the right side on one head, with the straight end aligned with the end of the dart. Right sides facing, pin the head pieces together. Machine-stitch the pieces together, leaving the neck open. Turn right side out and stuff.

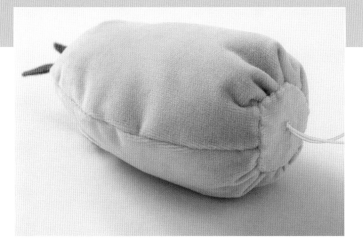

2 Run a gathering stitch around the neck opening and pull it up to approximately 6cm (2¹⁄₂in.) diameter. Thread the elastic on to the bodkin, double it and knot the ends with a large knot. From the back, take the elastic through a 7cm (3in.) circle. Turn under the edges of the circle and hand-stitch it to the gathered edge.

3 The larger circles need a hem to prevent fraying, so turn under 1cm (¹⁄₂in.) around the edge of each one and work running stitch all around. Pull up the thread tightly and secure it with a few backstitches to make Suffolk puffs. Gather the smaller circles in the same way, but without hemming them.

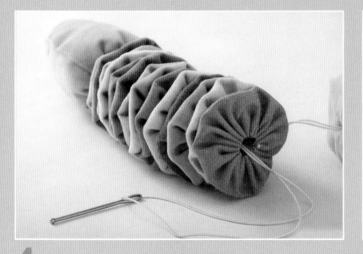

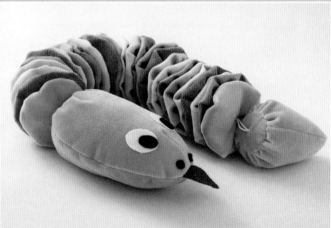

4 Thread the Suffolk puffs on to the elastic in whatever colour combinations you like.

5 Thread the elastic through the second 7cm (3in.) circle and knot it securely on the back. Right sides facing, machine stitch the tail pieces together. Turn right side out and stuff, adding a bell to give the snake a rattle in its tail. Make up the tail in the same way as the head, sewing the circle of fabric to the gathered opening. Glue felt eyes and nostrils to the snake's head. If you're worried about the eyes and tongue becoming detached, sew running stitch around them in a similar colour to the felt.

piles of pillows

Scatter cushions in different fabrics not only offer great seating for a child, they also look attractive when arranged together.

pattern

If you are drawn to and love pattern, then be bold with it in some areas of the room. As with vibrant colour, filling the space with pattern wouldn't be a good idea in a nursery for such a young child, but confined to certain areas it works wonderfully well. The hot-pink curtains with their gold foliage motifs are an interesting example of this. Being window-sill length rather than floor length, they are not big enough to dominate the room, and they frame the view through the window brilliantly.

Cushions provide another way of introducing pattern into the room. Made from a mixture of plain and printed fabrics, the smaller multi-coloured scatter cushions add lively splashes of pattern, while the more muted colours of the larger cushions and bean bag blend with the cot and pale wood floor. The same muted pattern is used for the chair's slip cover (see pages 90–92 for instructions).

The third main area where pattern is used is in the big mural on the wall opposite the cot. The shapes, cut from a selection of wallpapers, feature a variety of patterns and colours. The pale green painted background prevents the motifs detracting from one another and keeps the overall effect looking fresh, rather than too intense.

storage

The two big, built-in wardrobes have shelving as well as hanging space and all of the child's clothes and most toys can be stored away in them. Two shelves on the wall above the cot provide more space for soft toys and books, and there is enough floor space to keep larger toys, such as an old-fashioned wickerwork perambulator, out on show.

perfect cushions
While a chair cushion offers a great opportunity for stylish expression, it is primarily there for your comfort, so make sure it's one of your favourites.

pretty in pink
Bold and colourful curtains that are sill-length will act as an eye-catching feature but will not overwhelm the room. Make sure they are well lined to keep out the light when necessary.

chair cover

Chairs differ in size and dimensions but these general principles apply to all – look at the

diagram on page 131 to see how to measure your chair for a slip cover. Underneath this

pretty combo of printed linen and shocking-pink velvet is a tired and rather battered chair

that has been transformed into an altogether more glamorous piece for this stylish nursery.

You will need

- Diagram on page 131
- Two pieces of fabric, each measuring the height of the chair plus 3cm (1in.) by half the width of the back plus 13.5cm (5in.)
- One piece of fabric measuring the height and width of the front of the chair back plus 3cm (1in.)
- One piece of fabric measuring the width

and depth of the chair seat plus 3cm (1in.)
- Two pieces of fabric (side skirts) measuring the depth of the chair seat plus 9cm (3½in.) and the height of the seat from the floor plus 3cm (1in.)
- One piece of fabric (front skirt) the width of the chair seat at the front plus 15cm (6in.) by the height of the seat

from the floor plus 3cm (1in.)
- One piece of velvet measuring 22cm (9in.) wide and the height of the chair plus 3cm (1in.)
- Two pieces of velvet measuring 15cm (6in.) wide and the height of the seat from the floor plus 3cm (1in.)
- Pins, sewing machine and thread
- Six pieces of matching velvet ribbon

1 To make a back pleat, press under 11cm (4½in.) down one long side of each back piece of fabric. Open the pieces out flat and, right sides facing, pin them together. From the top, machine-stitch a 10cm (4in.) row down the pressed line. Open the seam out flat along the pressed lines.

2 Right side down, pin the larger piece of velvet to the back of the seam, aligning the raw edges all around. Machine stitch the velvet to both edges of the seam, continuing right down to the bottom of the fabric, taking a 1.5cm (½in.) seam allowance.

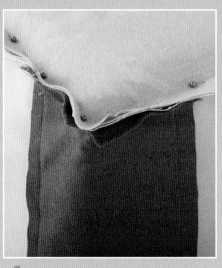

3 To make the front corner pleats, press under 7.5cm (3in.) on one long edge of each side skirt and both long edges of the front skirt. Right sides facing, pin a side skirt to the front skirt. Machine-stitch a 10cm (4in.) row down from the top and open out, as before. Pin and stitch one smaller piece of velvet to the back of the seam, as before. Attach the second side skirt to the other side of the front skirt and stitch on the velvet in the same way.

4 Wrong sides out, and using the diagram on page 131 as reference, pin all the pieces together over the chair, adjusting them for a snug fit. Sew all the pieces together, taking a 1.5cm ($\frac{1}{2}$in.) seam allowance all around.

5 Turn the cover right side out and place it on the chair. Pin up an even, narrow hem all around the bottom and stitch in place. Stitch ribbons to the inside of the back pleat for fastening.

comfortable chair

If you have a favourite chair, consider re-covering it rather than buying a new one for the nursery. The important factors are that the chair is comfortable enough to sit in for long periods, holding your child if necessary, and that the cover can be washed. Making a slip cover for a straight chair, such as the one in this room, is not difficult – but the simpler the chair, the easier the task, so if you want to re-cover an armchair, for instance, it may be better to get it done by professionals.

big bunny
Toys are part of any child's life and there is no reason why they shouldn't be part of your nursery design.

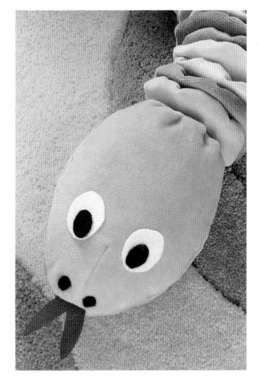

do it yourself
Making your own toys (see pages 86–8 for this snake) allows you to pick colours and patterns to suit the room they live in.

toys

If your child adores her soft toys and is happiest surrounded by them, incorporate them into the design of the room. They can sit in groups on the floor, or perch on cushions and chairs, and will help stamp your child's personality on the room. It can be tempting to buy just pretty toys if they are going to be displayed in this way, but remember that a child may not see what you see in a toy and might fall in love with the ugliest one imaginable. You should still put it out because, after all, it is her room.

wallpaper mural

Creating a mural using several different

wallpapers adds artistic style to the simplest

room. These wallpapers have designs with

an organic feel, so an imaginary landscape

that doesn't overpower the nursery works

beautifully with the papers and in the space.

You will need

- Templates on
  pages 132–5
- Wallpapers
- Wallpaper scissors
- Pasting table
- Wallpaper paste
- Damp cloth
- Acrylic jewels
- Contact glue

1 Using the templates and photograph (opposite) as guides if you wish, cut shapes from the wallpapers.

2 Lay each shape face down on the pasting table and brush the back of it with wallpaper paste. Stick the shape to the wall, smoothing it out with your hands. Wipe over the shape with the damp cloth to remove any excess paste.

3 Pick acrylic jewels in colours to complement the papers.

4 Put a dab of contact glue on the back of each jewel and stick each one to the wallpaper motifs to add detail and highlight areas.

spotty playroom

A dedicated playroom for your children does not have to be either large or permanent and will bring rewards for all concerned. Giving the children space to play in their own way allows you space in the house to pursue your own interests.

If you have a little-used dining room or a spare bedroom, consider turning it into a playroom for a few years. Is it possible to have the dining table in the kitchen or living room instead? How often do you have people to stay? Can the children share a room for the night so guests can use one of their bedrooms? Ask yourself these questions because while a playroom might sound like a luxury, it really can bring much-needed sanity into a home overflowing with children's toys and games. Remember that this option is suitable only if the children have reached an age where constant parental supervision is not necessary.

decorating

When planning this playroom, bear in mind that one day you will be able to reclaim it for its original purpose, so keep to a tight budget and don't splash out on anything that isn't strictly necessary. Paint the walls and either put in laminate flooring or sand and paint existing floorboards. As well as being practical – either way, the floor is quick and simple to touch up when it gets shabby – these options are easily changeable and inexpensive, and they certainly don't have to be boring.

play away
Children flourish in their own space, where they are able to play without worrying about causing damage.

the room

The secret of a successful converted playroom is flexibility. The room shown here was originally a dining room and, with a view to its becoming a dining room again in the future, it contains just one permanent feature – the radiator.

A large table with a melamine surface is an excellent idea. It can be used for crafts, cooking, games and homework, and for building dens under – a real multi-purpose piece. Cover it with oilcloth to incorporate it into the design scheme.

A big, inexpensive rug softens the hard flooring visually as well as physically, and a child-size armchair is fun. A smaller table and chairs, designed for children – not the type that folds up in case fingers get trapped – allow them to engage in different activities without annoying one another.

Large toys, such as the playhouse, often offer great value for space, and money, because they feature in all sorts of games. Freestanding storage units house craft materials and toys.

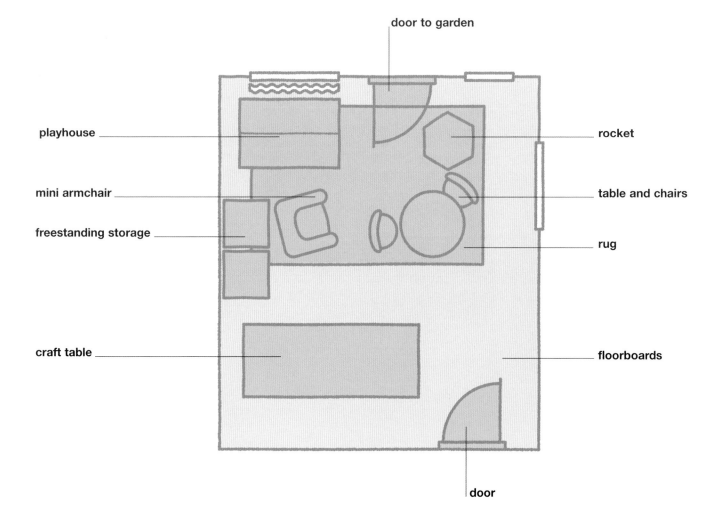

door to garden

playhouse

mini armchair

freestanding storage

craft table

rocket

table and chairs

rug

floorboards

door

creativity

Creative play is an important part of any child's development and can take so many forms. Most children love to cook, making fairy cakes or biscuits that, hopefully, will be as delicious as they look in the recipe book! A really practical playroom, where it doesn't matter if things get scratched or spilt, encourages children to paint and make models, sew and stage plays, and invent all sorts of complex games that amuse them so much.

In their imaginations, the big playhouse can be a camp, a hideaway or a shop, or it can be used as a reading room. On sunny summer days, it can be taken outdoors to add another dimension to games in the garden.

little cooks
The mixing of ingredients and decorating of cakes can be done by the children, but the cooking process needs adult supervision.

spotty walls

Decorate a focal wall with oversized designs for a fun feel in a playroom. I have used a neutral-coloured paint for the background and sample pots of bold pastel-coloured paints for the spots. Embellishing the spots with stencils and stickers makes the most of the simple circles.

You will need
- String
- Nail
- Pencil
- Hammer
- Wall filler
- Paint – use sample pots for the coloured circles
- Paintbrush
- Low-tack spray glue
- Stencil
- Stencil brush
- Stickers

1 Cut a piece of string the radius of the planned circle, plus about 10cm (4in.). Tie one end of the string to a nail and the other end to a pencil. Hammer the nail a little way into the wall where you want the centre of the circle to be. Keeping one finger on the head of the nail to hold it in place, stretch out the string and draw a circle around the nail.

As this is a room just for children, your painting doesn't have to be perfect – they won't notice the odd wobble or touched-in spot of paintwork. So have some fun yourself and experiment with different colours and shapes. If it all goes badly wrong, you can just paint over the mistakes and start again when the paint is dry. If you do this and the outline of the previous painted shape shows up as a ridge, a quick rub with fine-grain sandpaper will sort out the problem.

2 Remove the nail and use a dab of filler to cover the hole. Paint the circle, painting carefully just over the drawn line.

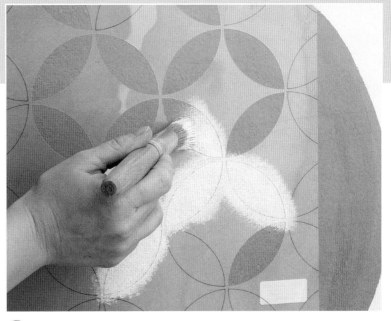

3 Spray the back of the stencil with glue and position it on the wall. Using the stencil brush and a stabbing motion, dab paint over the stencil.

4 As soon as you have finished painting, peel the stencil off the wall. Be very careful when doing this so that you do not smudge the paint.

5 Position the stickers where you want them. If they are the type with a transparent top sheet, leave that in place, smooth each sticker down, then peel off the top sheet.

themes

If you are planning a theme, make it a generic rather than a specific one. A generic theme, such as spots, is less likely to date and become boring for the children, and is also less expensive – branded products with cartoon characters, for instance, are often costly. You can easily add to the theme with spotty cushions or curtains as you – and they – wish.

If you have boys and girls, make the theme gender-neutral or someone will feel that the space isn't really for them. Boys won't be happy in a fairy room and girls may be equally uncomfortable with camouflage patterns.

hold all
Canvas boxes that fit into a wooden or MDF unit provide excellent, flexible storage, and more units can be added as the need arises.

pop-print towels

sweetie cushion

A soft velvet centre between candy stripes creates a delicious alternative to a conventional cushion, and is easy to make. I've used new fabric but this is a perfect project for re-using old soft furnishings. My wrapped sweetie cushion uses a bolster-shaped pad made with calico and polystyrene beans.

You will need

- 65 x 53cm (26 x 21in.) of calico or curtain lining for the inner pad
- Sewing machine and sewing thread
- Polystyrene beans
- 63 x 42cm (25 x 17in.) of velvet
- Two 63 x 21cm (25 x 8in.) pieces of striped fabric
- Sewing needle
- Ribbon
- Scissors

1 Fold the calico in half lengthways and, taking a 1.5cm (½in.) seam allowance, machine stitch the seam. Leave a 12cm (5in.) gap in the middle of the seam. With the seam at centre back, run gathering stitches across the ends. Pull the gathers up to measure 7cm (3in.) across, then machine stitch over them. Fill the pad with beans and sew the opening closed.

2 Right-sides facing and taking a 1.5cm (½in.) seam allowance, machine stitch a long edge of a piece of striped fabric to each shorter edge of the velvet.

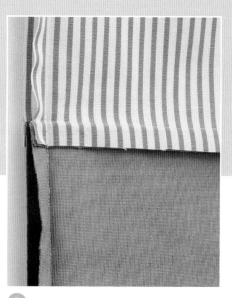

3 Right sides facing, fold the fabric in half lengthways. Taking a 1.5cm (½in.) seam allowance, machine stitch the long edges together to form a tube.

4 Turn under and machine-stitch a double 0.5cm (¼in.) hem around each end of the tube. Turn the tube right side out and slip the pad inside it.

5 Gather up the tube at either end of the inner pad. Fasten the gathers securely with a few stitches to hold them in place. Tie ribbon bows over the gathers.

light up
Plain lampshades can be covered in polkadot fabric to fit in with the design scheme (see pages 108–9).

so sweet
These bean bag covers echo the sweetie theme of the little bolster (pages 104–6).

furniture

Fun and flexible are the key words with playroom furniture. Bean bags are a great option because they can be moved around easily. Make sure the covers are removable and in a washable fabric. A big table that can be wiped clean is invaluable. This, plus storage, is all the furniture the children will really need. However, another table and chairs may help to avoid arguments, for avid readers extra shelving to accommodate their growing collection of books may be necessary, and a child-sized armchair is fun.

◀ **sitting comfortably**
You don't need much furniture in a playroom – some seating and a table are the only real essentials. Free floor space, giving room to play, is more important.

You will need

- Lampshade
- Sheet of paper large enough to
  make up a template of the shade
- Pencil
- Tape measure
- Pins
- Enough fabric to cover the shade
- Scissors
- Fusible webbing
- Iron
- Either a hot glue gun or UHU
  glue (optional)
- Pompom trimming (optional)

covered lampshade

Give an existing shade a new lease of life with this simple method of re-covering it. I like to use patterned fabrics to make the shades stand out from the plain versions, which are readily available. Choosing fabric remnants that co-ordinate or contrast with existing patterns and colours in the room can make for a dazzling result. Add a trimming as an optional extra if you want to embellish the shade.

1 Lay the shade on its side and roll it over the paper while drawing a line along the top and bottom rings. Add an additional 4cm (1½in.) at the top and bottom and along one side edge. Check that the template fits the shade and then pin the template to the fabric and cut it out.

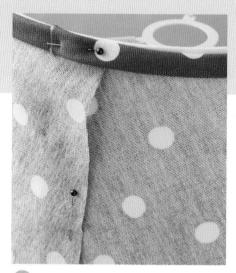

2 Right sides facing, fit the fabric over the lampshade, turning under the top and bottom edges. Adjust and pin the fabric until it fits the shade perfectly.

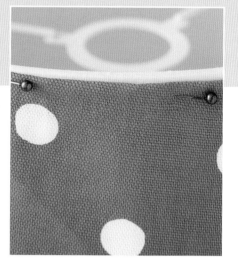

3 Use fusible webbing to hold the hems in place. Iron it down following manufacturer's instructions. Then glue the fabric to the shade, applying the glue to the backs of the hems only. Use pins to hold the fabric in place while the glue dries.

4 An optional extra touch is to glue pompom trimming around the bottom edge of the shade, again using pins to hold it in place while the glue dries.

fairy princess

If your little girl has always hankered after the ultimate fairy room, and you can indulge that wish, don't hold back on the detail. This magical bedroom is designed down to the smallest element to be a fairy princess's dream, a magical space just for her.

The delight and joy of this room is that every part of it enters into the flower fairy theme. From the fabulous bed to the step needed to get into it, from the miniature grandfather clock to the hairbrush, the attention to detail is all-encompassing. With a popular theme such as fairies, it is not difficult to achieve – there are plenty of products you can buy to enhance the look. This may not be a whole bedroom to consider if you are on a tight budget, but it is the most wonderful space, and even if you create just a fairy corner, it will be a haven for a little girl who loves all things pink and pretty.

dream

For many mothers this room won't be just an indulgence for their daughter, it will be a dream come true for them, too. Whether they aspired to a flower fairy room as a child and never had that wish fulfilled, or whether the child in them has never grown out of the 'fairy phase', many big girls are as susceptible to this room as little girls are. The only issue a mother will have to face is losing her secret dream room when her little girl grows up and, having had her fairy wishes answered, moves on to want a teenager's room with groovy wallpaper, pop posters and a futon bed.

fairy tale
A miniature sofa covered in the prettiest fabric is the perfect place to sit and daydream.

A painted chest of drawers is charming as well as providing practical storage space.

little friends
Soft toys can live happily in this magical room, sitting in front of a treasured mother and daughter photograph.

design details
Minor elements, such as paper drawer liners and the little girl's hairbrush, fit into the theme.

storage

Just because a room is pretty doesn't mean it's not practical. In fact, the prettier it is, the more storage you need so that everyday items can all be tidied away. This flower fairy room has loads of storage in the shape of two chests of drawers and a wardrobe with double-height rails for all the clothes, shelving for books, an under-basin cupboard and a capacious hidden storage unit under the window seat to hold larger toys and games.

the room

This bedroom is quite full of furniture and so is more of a place to relax and to sleep than it is a playroom, although if there's space, a table and chairs would be well used. The four-poster bed is easily the largest piece and, occupying a central position, sets the style for the whole room.

All the furniture has been chosen for looks as well as practicality and some pieces, such as the miniature grandfather clock, are pure frivolity, and yet so charming.

Architectural features, such as the bay window and fireplace, have been considered part of the design. A hand basin is a great idea in a little girl's room and helps ease the bathroom rush in the morning.

The dressing table holds trinkets and accessories, while shelves built in above it offer space for books. A sofa, covered in flower fairy fabric, in front of the window gives the room a 'grown-up' feel that an aspiring princess will appreciate.

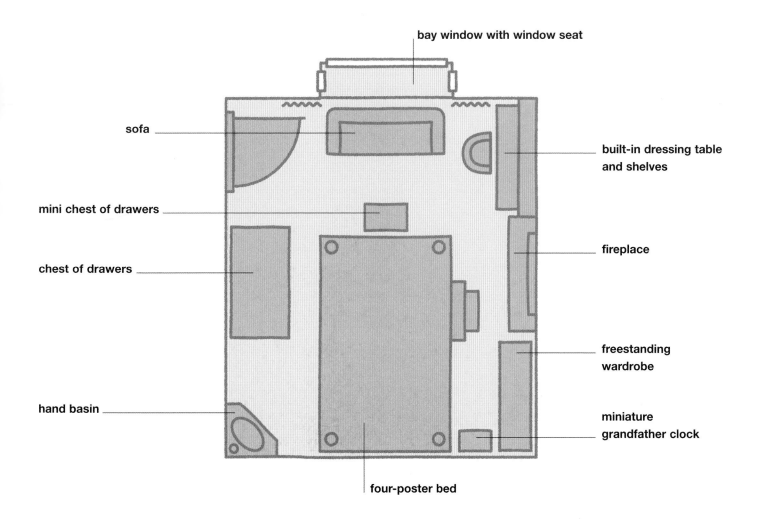

bay window with window seat

sofa

built-in dressing table and shelves

mini chest of drawers

chest of drawers

fireplace

freestanding wardrobe

hand basin

miniature grandfather clock

four-poster bed

sleep

This is a full-sized single bed with four-poster curtains and a tented canopy, although the curtains are dress only – they don't close. The bed is higher than usual and so a step is provided for climbing in and out. The bedspread and some scatter cushions are made in the same fabric as the four-poster curtains, which are lined in pretty gingham for a thoroughly co-ordinated look. The final effect is certainly grand, but it is also cosy, and the fabric choices mean that it doesn't look out of place for a young lady's room.

No matter how stylish the bed, it has to be comfortable and practical as well, and this one really is. The pulled-back curtains don't interfere with making up the bed. The patterned bedspread means that plain duvet covers and pillowcases work perfectly well. The curtains can be taken down for cleaning if need be, but the best way to keep them fresh is to untie the bows and vacuum the curtains and canopy with the vacuum-cleaner extension.

colours

When choosing such a strong theme, you do need to be careful about colours. Getting the balance right between sweet and sickly can be tricky. The fabric used in this room sets the overall colour choices, with the green of the foliage lifting the pinks of the flowers and fairies. The palest pink walls and off-white carpet, the off-white furniture with scattered motifs and the introduction of bright pink accents and gingham to balance the flower fairy prints keep the look fresh and light. This is helped by the large windows, which let natural daylight flood into the room. Off-white is usually a better choice for a child's room than brilliant white, which can look hard and cold.

checked in
The bed canopy is fully lined with pleated and gathered gingham. The centrepiece is a magnificent Maltese bow.

take a bow
Dress bows made in two colours of gingham – pink and lilac – hold back the bed curtains. They can be unhooked from behind.

tooth fairy cushion

The magical tooth fairy who so cleverly takes lost teeth from under the pillow by night is beloved by all generations. The only difference between our grandparents' time and today is the amount of money that is left behind. A special tooth fairy cushion is a sweet and decorative addition to any fairy bedroom.

You will need

- Large, pale pink ric-rac
- Two 12.5 x 9cm (5 x 3½in.) pieces of pale pink linen
- Sewing machine and sewing thread
- 'Tooth fairy' label
- Sewing needle
- 33cm (13in.) square of pink velvet
- 7cm (3in.) wide strips of fabric, enough to make a frill to go right around the cushion
- 33cm (13in.) square of rosebud fabric
- 30cm (12in.) square cushion pad

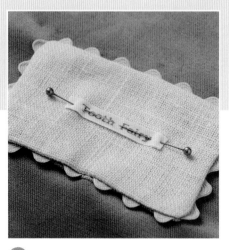

1 Machine stitch the ric-rac around the edges of one piece of linen, 1cm (½in.) in from the edges. Right side down, lay the second piece of linen on top of the first one. Taking the same seam allowance, stitch around the edges, leaving a 2.5cm (1in.) gap in one side. Turn right side out, press and slip-stitch closed.

2 Hand-sew the label to the centre front of the pocket. Then pin the pocket centrally to the pillow front and slip-stitch it along three sides, leaving the top edge open to create the pocket.

3 Taking narrow seam allowances, machine stitch the strips of fabric together to make one long length. Turn under and machine stitch a narrow double hem along one long edge. Pleat the raw long edge and machine-stitch over the pleats, 1cm (½in.) from the edge, to make a frill to fit around the cushion.

4 Right sides facing, pin the frill around the cushion front, aligning the raw edges. At the corners, snip the frill below the line of stitching and fold it over to turn the corner neatly.

5 Right sides facing, lay the square of rosebud fabric over the velvet. Taking a 1.5cm (½in.) seam allowance, machine stitch around the edges, leaving an opening in one side. Turn right side out, insert the pad and slip-stitch closed.

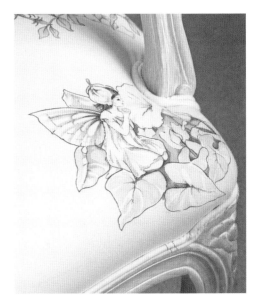

sitting pretty
The carved wooden frame of this little sofa provides a strong shape that is softened by the fabric upholstery.

flower fairy
On such a pale background, touches of apple green perfectly complement the delicate pinks of this delightful fairy.

inside edge
The gingham leading edge of the flower fairy curtains is a clever touch, showing how every element of this room has been considered.

pattern

Using one fabric print as the primary pattern in a room does solve a lot of design dilemmas – you don't need to worry about things co-ordinating and you have a specific pattern that accessories should match. However, there are some potential problems to watch for. In this room, the gingham fabric breaks up the flower fairy print beautifully. The checks sharpen and freshen the look while the gingham colours are sympathetic to it, and this is the secret of its success. Too much of any one pattern is always overwhelming, so you need to look for another to complement it.

butterfly coat hanger

The simplest ideas are often the prettiest – very little fabric and time are needed to make this ruched coat hanger, and it really does display the party dress delightfully. Recycle clothes destined to be thrown away and use different fabrics, from patterned cottons to soft velvets, to make a collection of hangers. The organza butterfly adds three-dimensional detailing, but you can sew on mini fabric rosebuds, a beautiful button or even a bejewelled brooch for a lovely finishing touch.

You will need

- Coat hanger
- 1.5cm (¹/₂in.) wide gros-grain ribbon the length of the hook, plus 1cm (¹/₂in.)
- Sewing needle and thread
- Strip of fabric twice the length of the hanger by the circumference, plus 4cm (1¹/₂in.)
- Iron
- Staple gun and staples
- Fabric with printed or woven motif
- Heavyweight fusible interfacing
- Small, sharp scissors

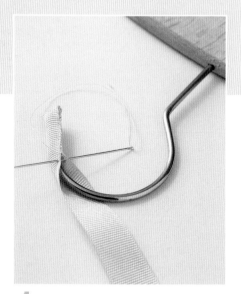

1 Turn under 1cm (¹/₂in.) at one end of the ribbon. Fold the ribbon in half around the coat hanger's hook and oversew the edges together. Secure the thread at the bottom of the hook.

2 Press under a 1cm (¹/₂in.) hem on each edge of the fabric. Fold the fabric in half lengthways around the hanger, with the hook in the middle. Starting in the middle, oversew the fabric edges together.

3 When you sew up the short ends of the fabric, roll the corners in and stitch them to create rounded ends.

4 Ruche the fabric along the hanger's length so that the ends of the hanger are tucked into the rounded ends of the fabric. As close to the end of the hanger as possible, put a staple into the wood to hold the ruching in place.

5 Iron the interfacing on to the back of the fabric with the motif, covering the whole motif. The interfacing stiffens the fabric and prevents the edges from fraying. Cut out the motif with sharp scissors and stitch it to the hanger at the base of the hook.

furniture

The wardrobe has two adjustable hanging rails, one above the other. The

clothes are not very long at the moment but, as the child grows and the

clothes get bigger, one rail can be removed to create full-length hanging

space. The two chests of drawers are different sizes – one full-size to hold

the child's clothes and one miniature, which can either be used to store

small items of clothing and accessories, or could be given over to the

clothes of favoured dolls.

dressed up

Arranging scatter cushions on the bed takes
just a few minutes in the morning and really can
add to the look of a room.

light

The curtains in this room are full-length, drawing straight across the bay window rather than following the shape of the bay. The pole extends well beyond either side of the bay so that the curtains can stack right back to let in as much light as possible. As in any child's room, curtains should ideally be lined, preferably with blackout lining, both for warmth and to help uninterrupted sleep during the day as well as at night.

on show
Don't hide pretty dresses away – display them on fabric-covered hangers (see pages 120–1) and make them a feature in the room.

shedding light
You can have lampshades covered in a fabric to match your scheme if the right ones are not commercially available.

fairytale mirror

This really is such a simple project and, at the same time, such a lovely one. Do allow the frosting spray to cure for a couple of weeks before cleaning the mirror, and for day-to-day cleaning a damp cloth is all that is needed. In time, the fairy can be removed by washing the mirror with a cloth and hot soapy water.

You will need
- Mirror
- Fairy stencil
- Masking tape
- Scrap paper
- Frosting spray
- Protective face mask

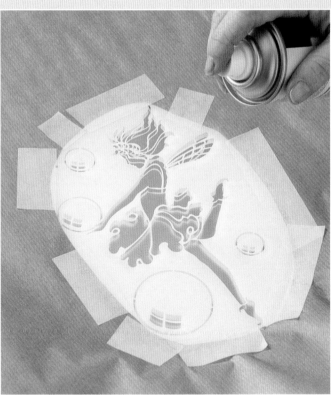

1 Working in a well-ventilated area (and wearing a protective face mask while actually spraying), lay the mirror face up on a level surface. Tape the stencil to the mirror.

2 Mask the rest of the mirror with scrap paper so that the frosting spray does not accidentally mark it outside the stencil. Cover the table or surrounding area if you are indoors, and then you are ready to start spraying. Apply two light coats of frosting spray, allowing the first one to dry for a few minutes before applying the second coat.

templates

pussycat toy, pages 14–16

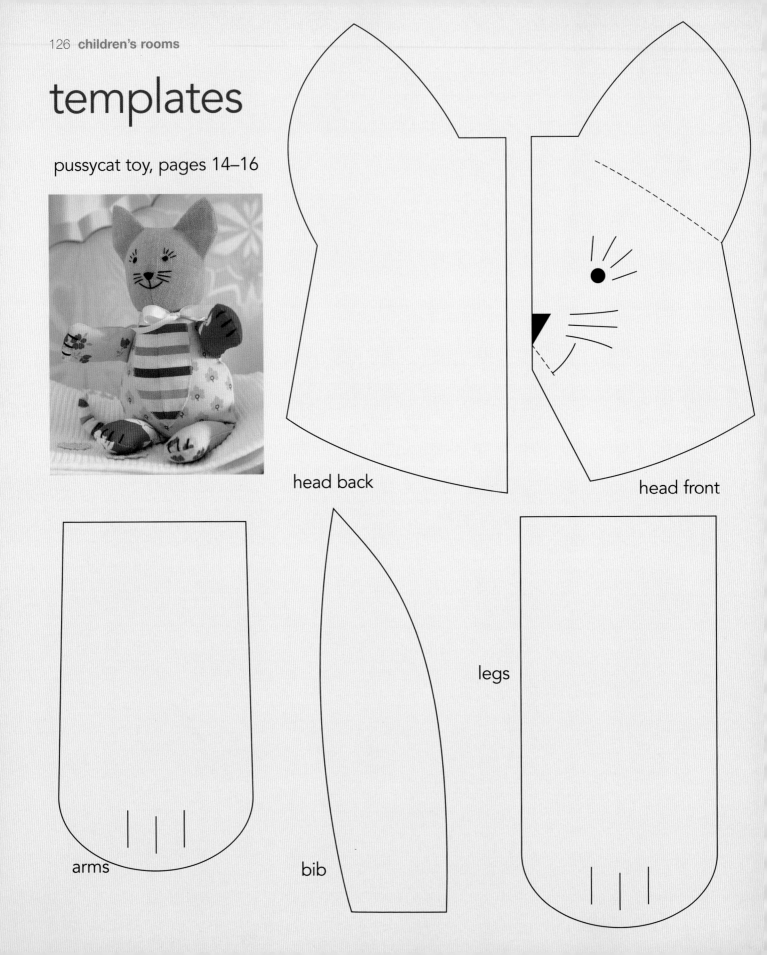

head back

head front

legs

arms

bib

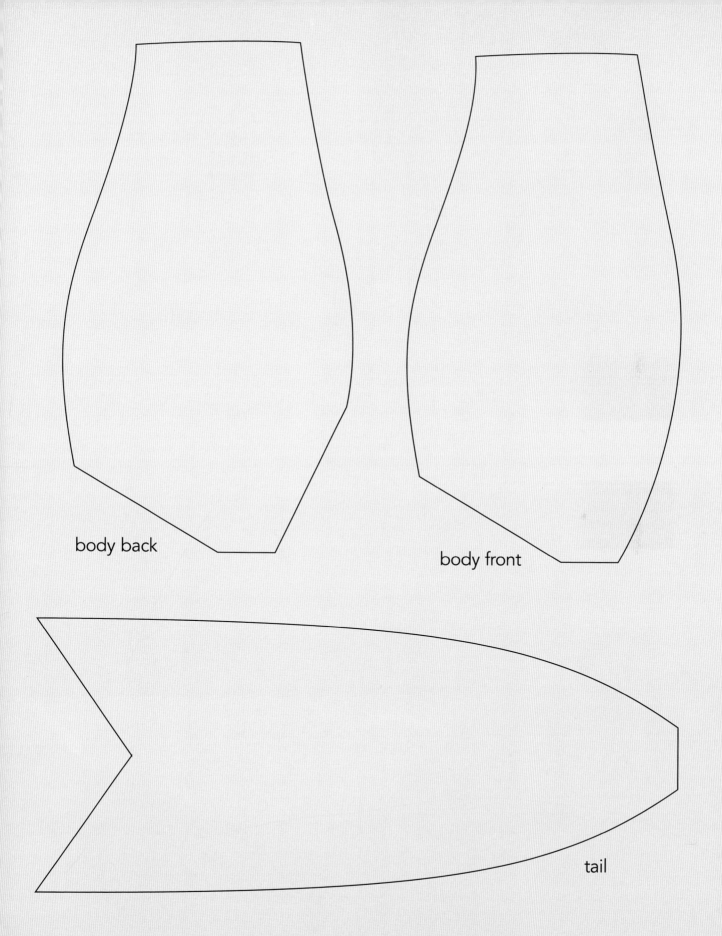

body back

body front

tail

building blocks, pages 26–7

fabric and photo bunting, pages 60–2

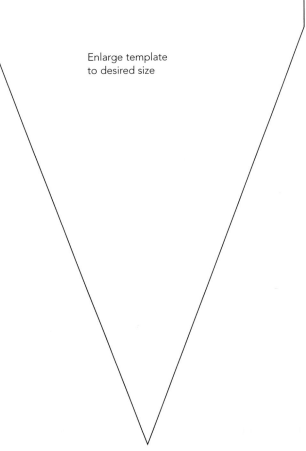

Enlarge template
to desired size

slot-together toy, pages 54–5

Follow the instructions on page 54 and check your first square against this diagram before making all of them

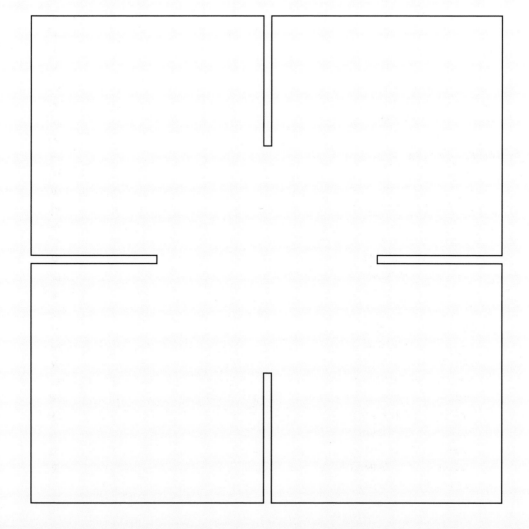

stretchy snake, pages 86–8

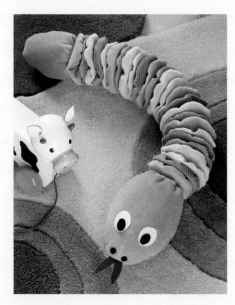

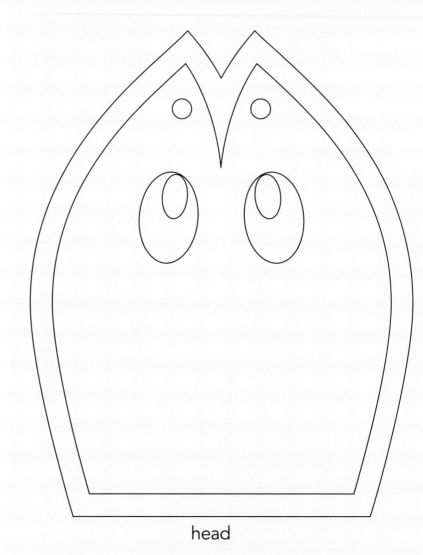

head

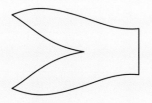

tongue

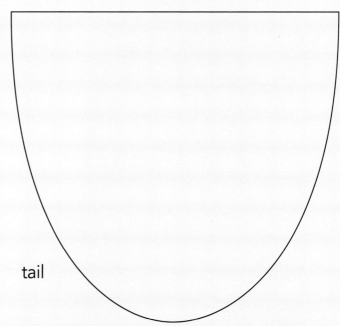

tail

chair cover, pages 90–2

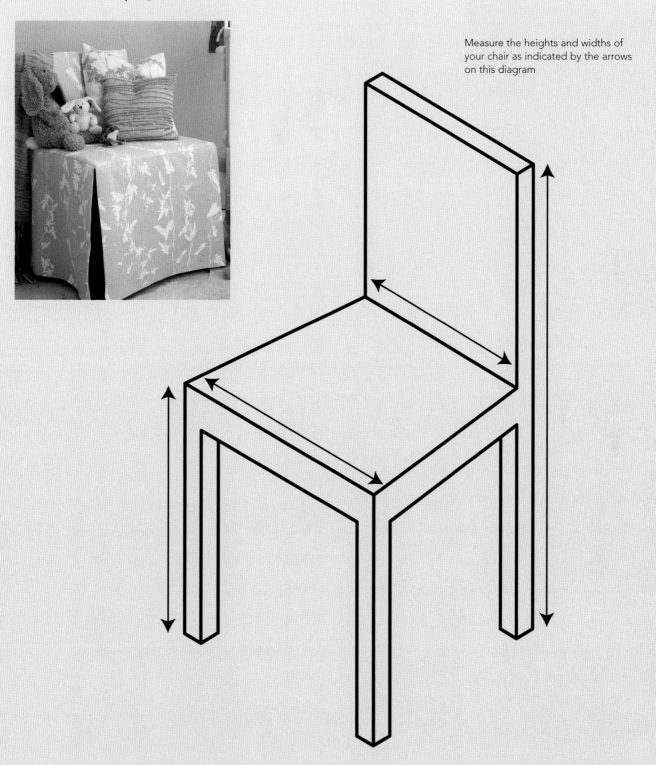

Measure the heights and widths of
your chair as indicated by the arrows
on this diagram

wallpaper mural, pages 94–5

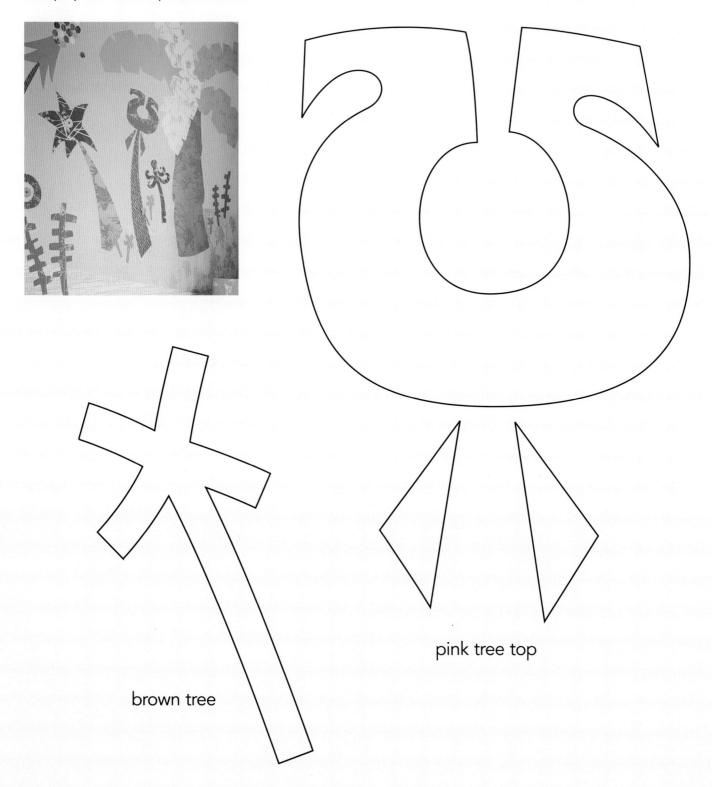

brown tree

pink tree top

blue star

blue tree

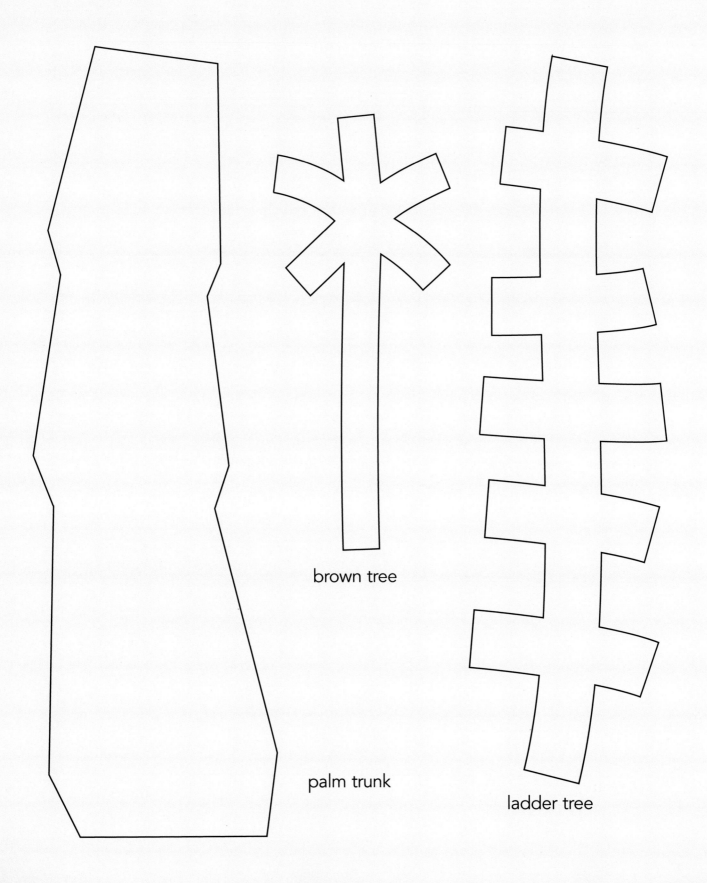

brown tree

palm trunk

ladder tree

ladder tree

palm leaf

suppliers

As an interior designer, I am in touch with an enormous number of suppliers, and of course I use products that are suitable for the work in hand. I hope this book has inspired you to choose a theme for your child's room and to have a go at transforming it yourself. Here's a list of suppliers of items for nurseries and children's rooms, all of whom have impressed me very much, and many of whom I used in this book's preparation.

Andrea Maflin
interior designer, author, artist and stylist
www.andreamaflin.co.uk

FURNITURE AND BEDDING

Aspace
Children's bedroom furniture and bed linen
www.aspaceuk.com

Babyface
Hand-quilted, luxury, themed bedding and soft furnishings for children
www.babyface.uk.com

Belle Maison
Painted furniture and co-ordinating accessories for babies and children. Chairs upholstered in your choice of fabric
www.bellemaison.co.uk

Blooming Marvellous
Furniture, clothes and toys for nursing mothers, babies and young children
www.bloominmarvelous.co.uk

Cosatto
Great range of nursery furniture, highchairs and bouncers
www.cosatto.com

Design Public
Alternative and unusual items for a modern lifestyle incorporating children's things
www.designpublic.com

Dormy House
Bedroom furniture for children's rooms, including a sleigh bed, folding screens, ottomans and mirrors
www.thedormyhouse.com

Earthlets
Organic products for babies and children including bedding, mattresses and washable nappies
www.earthlets.co.uk

Ellwood Haigh
Playscreens using designer fabrics, including a fairy castle, zoom rocket and soldier castle. The Petit Paravent range incorporates flame-retardant interliner, acrylic mirrors and fabric hinges
www.ellwoodhaigh.com

Feather and Black
Children's bedroom furniture plus fun bed linen, nightwear and accessories to match
www.featherandblack.com

Freckles
Gorgeous bedding includes hand-stitched coverlets and quilts, sheet sets and blankets from nursery to queen size.
www.freckles.com.au

Graham & Green
A curious mixture of all sorts of furniture for children's rooms
www.grahamandgreen.co.uk

The Great Little Trading Company
Brilliant storage solutions, furniture and toys for children
www.gltc.co.uk

Heather Spencer Designs
Quirkily themed children's furniture collections, including bugs, crazy pets, funky fairies, jungle, splash and barefoot in the park
www.hspencer.u-net.com

Ikea
Children's furniture and accessories
www.ikea.com

Jali

Custom-made radiator covers and furniture, including bookcases, cupboards and drawer units, made from MDF (ask to have them primed to make painting easier). Also suppliers of ready-made curtain pelmets, decorative folding screens and fretwork panels
www.jali.co.uk

John Lewis

Co-ordinating furniture and bedding for nursery and children's room, clothes, toys and more
www.johnlewis.com

JoJo Maman Bebe

Furniture, clothes and toys, including an organic range, for nursing mothers, babies and children
www.jojomamanbebe.co.uk

Kids Rooms

Children's bedroom furniture and accessories, available online only
www.kidsrooms.co.uk

The Kids Window

Furniture, clothes, personalized items and toys
www.thekidswindow.co.uk

Küster

Wooden nursery furniture and highchairs made from sustainable materials and manufactured to a strict ethical code
www.kuster.co.uk

Laura Ashley

Children's furniture, rugs, soft furnishings, fabrics, wallpapers, bed linen and accessories
www.lauraashley.com

The Linen Merchant

Children's themed bed linen, including rosebuds, safari and sailing away
www.thelinenmerchant.co.uk

Lionwitchwardrobe

Hand-crafted furniture and accessories, made in the UK
www.lionwitchwardrobe.co.uk

The Little Bedroom Company

Children's bedding and hand-painted wooden accessories
www.thelittlebedroomcompany.co.uk

Luma Direct

Organic blankets for cots and cot beds
www.lumadirect.com

M&S

Lovely, practical children's furniture and accessories
www.marksandspencer.com

Mothercare

A complete one-stop shop for kids from birth until eight years of age
www.mothercare.com

Next

Brilliantly designed and affordable bed linen, accessories and furniture for children
www.next.co.uk

NooNoo Designs

Personalized comfort blankets for babies
www.noonoodesign.com

The Nursery Window

Everything you need for your new baby, including nursery furniture and accessories
www.nurserywindow.co.uk

Oreka Kids

Wooden furniture finished with a clear, protective lacquer
www.orekakids.com

Puff & Pumpkin

Themed bedroom furniture and accessories
www.puffandpumpkin.co.uk

Rochingham

Mattresses for cot, cot bed and pram
www.rochingham.co.uk

Scumble Goosie

Gustavian-styled furniture and accessories
www.scumble-goosie.co.uk

Sia

Co-ordinating furniture and bed linen collections
www.sia-homefashion.com

Stompa Furniture

Specialists in innovative bedroom furniture for kids
www.stompa.co.uk

Sweetpea & Willow
Sophisticated, hand-carved furniture and soft furnishings for children's rooms
www.sweetpeaandwillow.com

VIP Kids
Themed children's beds (including the ultimate pirate bed), sofas and armchairs plus toy boxes and rocking horses
www.vipkids.co.uk

Viva Baby
Nursery furniture and accessories
www.vivababy.com

The White Company
Bedroom furniture, accessories and clothes for babies and kids – all in white
www.thewhitecompany.com

TOYS

Anne-Claire Petit
Lovely knitted soft toys
www.anneclairepetit.nl

Baileys
A superb range of soft toys and games
www.baileyshomeandgarden.com

Cox and Cox
Mail order site for children's craft products
www.coxandcox.co.uk

Dolls House Emporium
A leading supplier of doll's houses
www.dollshouse.com

Early Learning Centre
Everything to stimulate your child to learn and have fun from birth to ten years
www.elc.co.uk

Goffi
For Franck & Fischer soft toys and clothes by Kammakarlo
www.goffi.co.uk

The Hambledon
Brilliant children's toys and clothing
www.thehambledon.com

Helemill
Modern dolls houses, cots and bikes
www.helemill.com

Hibba Toys
Great selection of kids toys, games and toy boxes
www.hibba.co.uk

Holz Toys
Traditional wooden toys for babies and children
www.holz-toys.co.uk

Lapin & Me
Retro children's toys and textiles
www.lapinandme.co.uk

Letterbox
Educational toys, games and fancy dress
www.letterbox.co.uk

Paperpod
Toys and play furniture produced from recycled corrugated cardboard
www.paperpod.co.uk

Rainbow
Large scale climbing frames, playhouses including Tudor, Victorian, princess cottage and storybook bungalow, and trampolines with safety netting
www.rainbowplay.co.uk

Sleepover
Everything needed to keep the children entertained, including play-and-learn games
www.sleepovercompany.com

Toy-Choice
Wooden toys from fair trade manufacturers, using materials from sustainable sources
www.toy-choice.co.uk

Toy Tidy
Storage solutions for toys and clothes
www.toytidy.com

Urchin
Children's toys and activities
www.urchin.co.uk

The Win Green Company
Playhouses and accessories in 100% cotton
www.wingreen.co.uk

FABRICS, PAINTS AND ACCESSORIES

All Kids
Everything you could need for your child
www.allkids.co.uk

A Shade Above
Specialists in bespoke lampshades
www.ashadeabove.co.uk

Beasty Bags
Over-sized bean bags that resemble a
hippo, a rhino, a lion and an elephant
www.beastybags.co.uk

Baby Gadget Blog
Hunts around for new, innovative, fun,
sometimes wacky, highly functional and
smartly designed products for babies
and children. Completely compelling
www.babygadget.net

Bags of Love
This company will print your favourite
photo of your child on to a huge range of
items including bags, canvases,
blankets, cushions, wallpaper, roller
blinds, jigsaws and folding screens
www.bagsoflove.co.uk

Betta Care
Nursery products including bags,
bouncers and rockers, booster seats
and cribs, carriers and slings, foot muffs
and cosytoes, safety gates and fireguards,
strollers, joggers and support cushions
www.bettacare.co.uk

Berisfords Ribbons
Manufacturers of ribbons, bows and
trimmings
www.berisfords-design.co.uk

Caboodle Bags
Multi-award winning baby-changing bags
www.caboodlebags.co.uk

CanvasRus
Will transfer photos or your children's
drawings on to canvas
www.canvasrus.co.uk

Cath Kidston
Fabrics and accessories in vintage style
www.cathkidston.co.uk

Celia Birtwell
Charming designs from a design icon,
including fabric ranges suitable for
babies' and children's rooms
www.celiabirtwell.com

Clare Nicolson
Textiles combining digitally printed
cottons and silks with vintage fabric
www.clarenicolson.com

Copes
Traditional and modern curtain poles
www.copes.co.uk

Darling & Darling
Personalized accessories and rugs made
from your child's artwork
www.darlinganddarling.co.uk

Designers Guild
Upholstered furniture, wallpapers, paint,
fabrics and accessories for kids
www.Designersguild.com

Dream Genii
Pregnancy and feeding pillows, plus
aromatherapy products
www.dreamgenii.com

Dwell Studio
Baby bedding, hooded towels, buggy
blankets, bibs, soft toys in modern textiles
www.pomelo-london.com

Dylon
Easy to use fabric dye in many colours
www.dylon.co.uk

Earthborn Paints
Eco-friendly paints, varnishes and
woodwork products, including the
ProAqua range – oil and acrylic free,
with virtually no odour
www.earthbornpaints.co.uk

EcoCentric
Eco friendly products by Oliver Heath
www.ecocentric.co.uk

Ecos Organic Paints
Solvent free, environmentally friendly paints
www.ecospaints.com

Emma Bridgewater China
Collectible china for children, including
the much-copied polka dot and hearts,
men at work, dinosaur, circus and mice.
Also a practical melamine set
www.emmabridgewater.co.uk

55max
Will use one of your photos, or create a
montage, on fabric, blinds and wallpaper
www.55max.com

Greengate
Vintage fabrics and accessories
www.greengate.dk

Harlequin Harris
Affordable children's fabric
www.harlequinharris.com

Hillarys
All sorts of blinds
www.hillarys.co.uk

Hobbycraft
An invaluable source of craft materials
www.hobbycraft.co.uk

Ian Mankin
Multi-coloured ticking and other fabric
www.ianmankin.com

Jane Churchill
Classic fabrics for children's rooms
www.janechurchill.com

Jill Northam
Stunning fabrics made in Suffolk in the UK
www.jillnortham.co.uk

Jasper Conran
Upholstered furniture, fabrics, wallpapers,
paint and accessories
www.jasperconran.com

Les Louisettes
Innovative motifs for children's rooms
www.leslouisettes.com

Lullabys
Everything you need for bed and bath time
www.lullabys.co.uk

Malabar
Well-priced fabrics suitable for children
www.malabar.co.uk

Marimekko
Designs, manufactures and markets high-
quality clothing, textiles, bags and
accessories for children
www.marimekko.com

Modern Rugs
Affordable and washable rugs
www.modern-rugs.co.uk

Mothercare
A complete one-stop shop for kids from
birth until eight years of age
www.mothercare.com

Neisha Crosland
Stunning designs in wallpapers and fabrics
www.neishacrosland.com

NooNoo Designs
Personalized comfort blankets for babies
www.noonoodesign.com

O Ecotextiles
Emily Todhunter has collaborated with this
pioneering company to produce socially
and ecologically responsible fabrics
www.oecotextiles.com

Olicana
Cotton and wool fabrics, plain and striped
www.olicana.co.uk

Osborne & Little
Fabric ranges for children's rooms
www.osborneandlittle.com

Pedlars
Fun products for children
www.pedlars.co.uk

Plasti-kote
Frosting spray, easy to use and
removable
www.plasti-kote.co.uk

Purves & Purves
Original gift ideas for kids
www.purves.co.uk

Rice
Great storage solutions for toys and
children's things plus melamine crockery.
All Rice products are designed and
developed in Denmark, and produced in
the third world with respect for people
www.rice.dk

Romo
Affordable fabrics
www.romofabrics.com

Rufflette
Curtain poles and Universal Tempo
heading tape, designed for use with
any pole and track system
www.rufflette.com

Rugs Direct
Fun rugs for kids
www.rugsdirect.co.uk

Silvia Stickers
Huge range of silhouette designed stickers
www.silviastickers.com

Stencil Library
The world's leading designer of decorative stencils
www.stencil-library.com

Stickyups
Easy-to-apply, removable wall stickers
www.stickyups.com

Their Nibs
Textiles, bed linen and clothes for children from birth to ten
www.theirnibs.com

Villa Nova
Affordable fabrics
www.villanova.co.uk

Voyage
Innovative fabrics for children
www.voyagedecoration.com

Woven Labels
Woven labels of all kinds
www.wovenlabelsuk.com

CLOTHES

Aravore Babies
Incredibly soft clothes and bedding for babies and children made from fairly traded organic cotton and organic merino wool
www.aravore-babies.com

Aztec Store
Hand-made children's clothes and accessories for 0 to 8 year olds
www.aztecstore.com

Bambino Merino
Clothes and sleeping bags for babies made from soft, lightweight New Zealand merino wool
www.bambinomerino.com

Bumpto3
Innovative ideas for mothers from the early stages of pregnancy plus baby clothes, sleepwear and toys for babies
www.bumpto3.com

Christy
Ultra soft and absorbent children's towels, robes and snuggle sets
www.christy-towels.com

Couverture
Clothes and toys for babies and children
www.couverture.co.uk

Ej Sikke Lej
Inspired clothing for children

Hjorth Copenhagen
Children's clothes
www.hjorth-cph.dk

Lollipop
Washable nappies made from a wide range of materials including soft breathable cotton, quick-drying polar fleece, super absorbent micro fibre, organic cotton and bamboo. The site is full of information and advice
www.teamlollipop.co.uk

Lula Sapphire
Eco-friendly clothes for babies and children, cribs, bedding and toys
www.lulasapphire.com

acknowledgements

boho chic

Location provided by Andrea Maflin. www.andreamaflin.co.uk

Baskets, Matalan; bed linen, Mothercare; birds, Clare Nicholson (for wall), Matalan (for mobile); blackout blind, Mothercare; blankets, Aztec, Mothercare, the White Company; chair, Laura Ashley; chest of drawers, Mothercare; clothes, Aztec, Mothercare, the White Company; coat hanger, Ann Petit, the White Company; cot, Mothercare, the White Company; curtains, Malabar; cushions, Clare Nicholson; decorative extras, Matalan, Clare Nicholson, Laura Ashley, the White Company; fabric, Andrea Maflin (for baskets), Elanbach (for toy); fairy lights, the White Company; lace sheer, Laura Ashley; lamp, Laura Ashley; nappies and baby bits, Mothercare; panelling, B&Q; panelling wallpaper, Neisha Crosland; panelling paint, Sanderson; peg wallrail, Mothercare, the White Company; picture frames (family tree), Matalan; pouffe, Ann Petit; ribbons (for baskets), Berisfords; rug, Aztec; side table, the White Company; tie back, Laura Ashley; toys, Ann Petit, Clare Nicholson, the White Company; vintage mirrors, Andrea Maflin; wallpaper, Jocelyn Warner

vintage style

Location provided by Petra Boase. The fabric prints/canvases, knitted teddies and Florence's T-shirt are Petra Boase designs. Her eclectic range of products include hand-made greetings cards, babies' T-shirts, boldly printed kitchen textiles, flocked photo albums and stationery. www.petraboaseshop.com

Badge and magnet kits, Hobbycraft; bed and valance, the White Company; chair and notice board fabric, Ian Mankin; chair and other vintage fabrics, auction houses via www.localauctioneers.co.uk; clothes, Aztec, Lapin & Me, Mothercare, the White Company; cushions, Jane Churchill (fabrics for back), John Lewis (pads, kits for fabric-covered buttons), Liberty (patterned fabrics for letters), Olicana (fabrics for front); desk and chair, Scumble Goosie; paint, Earthborn; toys, Lapin & Me, Early Learning Centre; varnish, Polyvine

eco nursery

Location provided by Chic Shack; also armchair, bed cover, chest of drawers, cot bed, cushions, shelf with hooks. Chic Shack has an extensive and versatile range of painted furniture and offer a made to measure service. www.chicshack.net

Button heart and letter stamp kit, Cox and Cox; embroidered blanket, Luma; fabric (to trim rug), Celia Birtwell; keepsake frames, Ikea; paint, Ecos Paints; rug, the White Company; stickers, Stickyups

outdoor den

Location provided by Chic Shack; also furniture and accessories. www.chicshack.net

Bean bag fabrics, Designers Guild; beans, John Lewis; bespoke rug, Darling and Darling; eyelets, John Lewis; fabric pockets, Cath Kidston (cowboys), Ian Mankin (red check), Jane Churchill at Colefax & Fowler (blue stripe), Malabar (blue plain); flags, Jane Churchill at Colefax & Fowler (blue stripe), Jill Northam (Ahoy and Stripy Jack), Olicana (red/white ticking), Osborne & Little (green stripe), Romo (plain), Villa Nova (electric blue and electric green), 55max (photographic); ribbons, Berisfords; toys, Lula Sapphire

room to grow

Location provided by The Children's Furniture Company. Furniture is from their award-winning Tutti Frutti range for nursery and children's rooms. www.the childrensfurniturecompany.com

Blinds, Hillarys; canvas, canvasRus; curtains, Designers Guild (stripy), Marimekko (large bowl with fruit, green house, black tree trunks); curtain pole and tempo heading, Rufflette; duvet covers, the White Company; fabric dye, Dylon; globe, urchin; paint, Ecos Organic Paints; rug, Orc Interiors; stencil (spaceman), the Stencil Library; varnish, Polyvine

nursery colour

Location provided by Clarissa Hulse; also main fabric, curtain fabric and wallpapers for mural. Clarissa Hulse is well known for her exquisite cushions and wraps and her wonderful sense of colour. www.clarissahulse.com

Bedding, Lula Sapphire; **blackout lining**, John Lewis; **chair fabric**, Villa Nova; **comforter**, NooNoo Design; **gems**, Hobbycraft; **rug**, Rugs Direct; **snake toy fabric**, Villa Nova

spotty playroom

Location provided by Andrea Maflin. www.andreamaflin.co.uk

Animal stuffed toys, GOFFI; **apron fabrics**, Cath Kidston, Greengate; **armchair**, VIPS kids; **bean bag fabrics**, Designers Guild (green faux suede), Greengate (brown and cream polkadot), Villa Nova (blue velvet, yellow brushed cotton); **cardboard rocket**, Paperpod; **chalkboard table and chair**, Lula Sapphire; **curtain fabric**, Greengate (spotty and ivory fabric), Romo-Linara (ivory brushed cotton); **lampshade**, A Shade Above; **lampshade fabric and pompoms**, Cath Kidston; **playhouse**, the Win Green Company; **storage**, the Great Little Trading Company; **sweetie floor cushions fabric**, Cath Kidston (pale blue polkadot), Greengate (navy and ivory spot), Villa Nova; **paint**, Earthborn; **stencils**, the Stencil Library; **stickers**, Stickyups; **toys**, Early Learning Centre

fairy princess

Location provided by Dragons of Walton Street; also all furniture and accessories. Their beautifully hand-painted furniture can be personalized to reflect your child's interests. www.dragonsofwaltonstreet.com

Fabrics (for tooth fairy cushion), Harlequin Fabric (striped border), Jill Northam (mini rosebud on reverse) Villa Nova (shocking-pink velvet, pocket); **frosting spray** (for the mirror), Plasti-kote; **labels** (tooth fairy), Woven Labels; **ric rac trim**, Colefax & Fowler; **wallpaper** (lining for chest of drawers), Colefax & Fowler

Spending time with children is joyful. They have such an immediate and instinctive honesty, they want to investigate and learn, and most importantly, they embrace the moment. I know each of us could learn a lot from them, and I'm grateful to all little people who have inspired me over the years.

A number of talented individuals have played such an intrinsic part in the production of this book that they all deserve a mention. A big thank you to everyone at Cico Books. I want to thank Cindy Richards especially for giving me the opportunity to write this book; the inexhaustible enthusiasm of Kate Haxell and her patient editing; the dedication and calm of Sally Powell for putting it all together. I'm also extremely grateful to Chris Drake for his creative photography and for many amusing and intense days spent together; the kind and encouraging Marion Paull; and the effervescent Sonia Pugh. I'm indebted to Claire Legemah for the design and Stephen Dew for the artworks.

Heartfelt thanks go to all the property owners who allowed us into their stylish and inspiring homes – without you this book would not have been possible. To Sarah Codrington, the owner of the Children's Furniture Company, who allowed me free rein to do whatever I wanted in her home; Maria and Gary Myers of Chic Shack – your generosity and kindness is breathtaking; the incredibly talented Clarissa Hulse and her team, not forgetting her daughter Anjelica, who made the nursery come alive; dearest Lynn and Tom for allowing me to borrow their three children, Jessica, Olivia and James, who are such a delight, for the spotty playroom; Lucinda Croft and her daughter Phoebe and the entire team from Dragons of Walton Street, who made the fairy bedroom of dreams, so beautifully – I felt like one of the family; Lord and Lady Elspeth Horden – you made us feel so at home, a day to remember; the excitable and creative Petra Boase and her darling Florence, whose home and whole way of life is inspiring; dearest James and Susie for allowing me to initiate your baby daughter Amy into modelling, and what a sweetie, she's a natural. Personal thanks go to my dear friends Lucy Wrisdale, who worked with me in the making of this book, and Lucinda Moodie – special friends come along only a few times in a lifetime; the one and only Beryl Miller, modest by nature but a magician with anything to do with fabric – you've been an incredible support throughout this book and a pillar of strength; finally, my darling companion in life, Paul, for his unfailing support and friendship and belief in me.

index